GAY RIGHTS
TRANS RIGHTS

A psychiatrist/lawyer's 50-year battle

RICHARD GREEN MD JD

HOMOSEXUALITY

It was the most successful event in public health history. Four million Americans were cured of the same illness, all at once. In 1973, the American Psychiatric Association agreed (with some of us) that homosexuality was not a mental illness. Our battle was won, but the war for gay rights continued.

In a landmark 1974 court case, I testified for a woman living as a lesbian who fought for child custody after divorce. Our victory was dampened by subsequent losses.

When I advocated same-sex marriage on a US television debate in 1974, few viewers thought they would see that as reality. It took three decades.

I challenged "the face on the Florida orange", evangelist singer Anita Bryant in her anti-gay crusade of 1977. She championed a referendum to deny equal rights for gays in Miami. The discriminatory law was approved 2-1. It would be two decades before this was repealed.

My twenty-five-page legal document in 1987 on behalf of a gay man trying to serve in the US military was unsuccessful. It would be two decades before this ban was reversed.

When I challenged the Boy Scouts (in my first trial as an attorney in 1990) for refusing to appoint a gay teenager as a scout leader we lost. It would be two decades before a change in Scout policy.

When Colorado passed a law denying gays and lesbians equal protection in 1992, I testified for its repeal. That time we won at the US Supreme Court.

TRANSSEXUALISM

I wrote letters for American patients to foreign surgeons recommending what was then called "sex-change surgery" in 1965 because no US medical center was helping the transsexual.

The strength of resistance from American doctors to transsexual treatment was demonstrated by my questionnaire sent to hundreds of physicians. The majority of psychiatrists and surgeons would condemn a transsexual to likely suicide rather than enable sex reassignment.

The breakthrough occurred in 1966 when a handful of us referred transsexual patients to The Johns Hopkins Hospital. When this prestigious medical center performed their surgery, transsexual treatment was legitimized.

As treatment became increasingly available, I testified in court from the 1970s to enable transsexuals to progress in their new life. As with gays and lesbians, they were challenged in employment and parenting.

A commercial airline pilot with many years' flight experience as a man took medical leave and tried to return to pilot as a woman. The airline refused.

A schoolteacher wanted to return to work after completing transition from a man to a woman. The school refused.

During gender transition to live as a woman, the divorcing father of a four year old daughter sought continued parental contact. The mother insisted that the father must appear as a man.

A man, born female, married a woman and the couple adopted children. For years they had sexual intercourse, always while the man wore a prosthetic penis. When the relationship failed, the wife insisted that she never knew that the penis was artificial, or that the man had been born a woman. The marriage was invalid because, at the time, two persons born female could not marry. She demanded that he have no further contact with the children as he was neither their legal nor their biological father. I argued psychological parenthood. This was the only father the children had known.

These court cases were often bitter. As with gays and lesbians, sometimes we won.

WHAT THIS BOOK IS:

WHAT FOLLOWS WAS COMPILED FOR ADAM HINES-GREEN, PREVIOUSLY TRAINED IN MEDICINE, NOW OCCUPIED WITH ART. NEARLY ALL THAT IS DESCRIBED HERE TRANSPIRED BEFORE HIS BIRTH.

A REGRET OF NOT HAVING A CHILD UNTIL AGE 53 IS NOT KNOWING ENOUGH OF HIS LIFE. THAT VOID CANNOT BE REMEDIED AT ALL. ADAM'S VOID FOR MINE CAN BE REMEDIED SOMEWHAT BY WHAT FOLLOWS.

IF OTHER READERS FIND THESE SKIRMISHES IN THE BATTLE FOR GAY AND TRANS RIGHTS INTERESTING, THAT IS A BONUS.

WHAT THIS BOOK IS NOT:

WHAT FOLLOWS IS NOT ABOUT THE HISTORY OF THE GAY AND TRANS CIVIL RIGHTS MOVEMENTS. IT IS ABOUT THE 50-YEAR ROLE OF ONE PERSON, TRAINED IN PSYCHIATRY AND LAW. HISTORY BOOKS WILL FLESH OUT THE CONTEXTS OF THESE BATTLES. THEY WILL DESCRIBE THE EFFORTS OF OTHER ACTIVISTS. WHAT FOLLOWS IS A HISTORY OF MY TIME, NOT A HISTORY OF THE TIMES.

WHAT FOLLOWS

PART 1
HOMOSEXUALITY

7

PART 2
TRANSSEXUALISM

Part 1

HOMOSEXUALITY

ONE

MOMMY WOULDN'T LET ME PUSH A BABY CARRIAGE

Now, at 81 years, I am still asked: "Why did you choose this career? Why were you battling for the rights of homosexuals and transsexuals from the mid-1960s?"

To help answer that, I go back to earlier experiences. One trigger was a summer theater company just before medical school in 1957. To my shock, I was the only heterosexual actor. Before then, I didn't know any homosexual people, or so I thought. But, in the next year, had a professor not adopted me to start my sex and gender research into the origins of homosexuality, that theater trigger could have fired a blank. A second trigger was when exposure to homosexual doctors and others (as psychologically healthy or unhealthy as I was) fuelled my energy to fight the "homosexuality is mental illness" doctrine.

And the third was when I witnessed the pain of the medically-orphaned transsexual patients of the physician Harry Benjamin in the 1960s, when no one else would help them.

Earlier childhood seeds may have germinated from this feed of summer theater, gay friends, and Harry's medical office.

I am about four years old. My mother is exiting the bathroom turning right toward the bedroom, wearing nothing below her waist. As she turns I see her buttocks. I comment (I cannot remember what I said). My dad responded, "He's starting early." Step One toward sexuality.

Around the same time, I am in the street with my mom, and a little girl and her mom. The girl is pushing a child's size baby carriage, called a "pram" in England. I shove her away and try to push it. My mom scolds me, "No, that is for girls." She could have said, "No, that's not yours." Step One toward gender.

My first gift as an infant was a football. I learned this decades later when my dad died and I helped my mom clean out his possessions. I read my baby book. Dad had been captain of his high school football team. He wanted me to follow into sports. But, at practice ordeals with him as a little kid, I could never handle that pigskin-covered obese sausage. I couldn't get my fingers to grip the laces to throw it. I let him down. Later, my parents scraped together enough money to send me to summer camp away from the Brooklyn 90-degree temperature and 90-percent humidity (no air conditioning in rent-controlled tenements). There, at the start of summer, I overheard my dad asking my counsellor to work on my sports. To no avail.

(The genes for sports skill must skip generations. My son was captain of his high school football team.)

I was a "sissy". Not the same as those feminine boys described in my research study, decades later, of boys who became gay men. No cross-dressing, doll play, playing mother in mother-father games. Only one feature qualified me as a sissy: terrible at sports.

I let my dad down, but I would make it up. I had a hidden asset. One day, at school, we were given IQ tests. My dad had a second job, and taught at night school to earn a bit more. He met my teacher who was also teaching there. He was told, "Your son is a genius." So, I didn't have to be cajoled into academic success, as depicted in the cartoon Jewish family. I could make him proud.

Years later, as "my son, the doctor", I played to an audience of one. In 1970, I told my dad that I had just signed on to edit a new journal, *Archives of Sexual Behavior*. The next day he subwayed to the publishing office in lower Manhattan to sign up for a subscription. The receptionist at Plenum Press, which published a hundred journals, had no idea what he was talking about. Eventually, my publisher appeared and shook his hand. Dad became Subscriber Number One. It didn't matter that I couldn't throw that fat sausage.

Championing sex and gender underdogs was predated for me by rooting for the hapless baseball team that played at Ebbets Field (a few streets down from my small apartment) -- The Brooklyn Dodgers. The crowd roar from night games and the stadium lights kept me awake most of the pre-midnight hours all summer. The Dodgers were legendary also-rans. "Wait'll next year" was their mantra. This was reminiscent to the millions of Jewish residents in Brooklyn of the mantra, "Next year in Jerusalem", the promised return to the Holy Land.

I was unaware of that religious mantra, though. I was not raised as a religious kid. My friends went to Hebrew school every day after state schooling. They went to synagogue, at least on high holy days, and perhaps for the weekly Sabbath. Remarkably, for parents born in 1909, mine were atheists.

When WWII ended in 1945, and **LIFE** magazine portrayed the skeletons, some living, at the Nazi concentration camps, I did not understand that most of them were Jews, some perhaps relatives I had never met. Later, I realized that I had won the geographic birth lottery by being born in Brooklyn, not Berlin.

All the kids at my grade school were Jewish. My first lesson in anti-Semitism was at age 11. My dad drove us in our new 1947 Ford out to the suburbs for a Thanksgiving meal. We passed a billboard advertising a new post-war housing development. The sign announced, "For Class A Citizens Only". My dad said, "That means no Jews." My second was a few years later when I arrived at university on scholarship. I was chatting with another freshman in our dorm during the first week. He told me that he was surprised when he saw me and learned that I was Jewish. "I thought Jews had horns."

As a pre-medical student studying furiously for admission to med school (where there were far more applicants than open places), I learned much more about anti-Semitism. As it neared application time, I found out that there was a ten per cent maximum Jewish quota in med schools. Only a few years after the terrors of the Holocaust were revealed, in a country that helped defeat the Nazis (who barred all Jews from medical school), it was legal to bar some.

As my identity was consolidating as a minority, an outsider, an underdog, my personal life reflected this position at the edge. Inter-racial dating was taboo in 1954.

At university, I was assisting at an orientation meeting for freshmen and (thankfully) "freshwomen." Sitting halfway back in the meeting room was a girl who did not look like anyone I had ever seen. Beautiful, exotic, brown. I stared at her. Yolanda stared back. She was from San Juan, Puerto Rico.

At the end of the year, my indelible first love left school. A year later she married someone else. I desperately wanted her back. In two years she divorced. She found me during my second year at med school and we re-united.

My rich lawyer uncle who had been helping support me through school cut me off financially for marrying "a schvartze" (a black). So, I worked at the dormitory switchboard to earn money (one of those contraptions with a hundred wires to be plugged in to connect a call). Yolanda was my wife at a med school where there were no black students, and the quota of seven Jewish students (the magnificent seven).

As my psychiatry interest was taking shape, my identity as minority, outsider, underdog embraced other minority outsider underdogs: the homosexual and the transsexual.

Inevitably, there were those who were convinced that my professional interest in sex and gender was symptomatic of an underlying conflict over homosexuality. Freud described sublimation as a psychological defense whereby an unacceptable impulse is unconsciously converted into socially acceptable action.

On the panel with me for my first professional paper at the 1968 American Orthopsychiatric Association meeting in Chicago was a prominent psychoanalyst, Joe Noshpitz. For my talk, I was hung over. I had been up one way or another most of the night with a lady grad student from the University of Chicago. After I struggled through my paper on the feminine boys I had been studying in a research project, Noshpitz pulled me over. "After you have had your analysis you will understand your homosexual roots that motivate you."

Hanna Fenichel, my analyst of three years, four days a week, never excavated that unconscious root. Nor did Noshpitz send me a bill.

Looking back at my career, it could have been more hazardous pursuing minority sex and gender causes had I been homosexual or transsexual. In addition to the stigma of having a mental disorder and the risk from criminal behavior, it would have been much easier to dismiss me with a clearing of the throat and a knowing smile.

But there were other risks. The unbridled enthusiasm and idealism of youth can result in shooting oneself in the foot (or scoring an "own goal"). I was contained by my protective mentors, John Money at Johns Hopkins and Robert Stoller at UCLA. In my university fortress, I had a less bloodied career fighting the sex and gender war than had I been a psychiatric practitioner out in the weeds, with my day job managing garden variety "tsoris" (troubles).

TWO

IN THE BEGINNING

The Old Testament pronounced the death penalty for a man who "lies with a male as with a woman." (1)

Two thousand years later, under English law, death by hanging for "buggery" was enacted by Henry VIII. This punished "the detestable and abominable Vice Committed with Mankind or Beast." (2)

By the 19th century, there were European sexual rights reformists, but their arguments went unheeded. The Hungarian Karl-Maria Kertbeny and the German Karl Heinrich Ulrich pioneered for rights and coined the term "homosexual" in 1868. They argued that these men and women should not be criminalized because homosexuality was inborn and not changeable. (3) *Psychopathia Sexualis* was the encyclopedia of 200 cases of variant sexuality compiled by the German Richard von Krafft-Ebing. (4) In his view, homosexuals could be well-functioning citizens and sodomy laws should be repealed.

Earlier than these reformists, however, was the English philosopher, Jeremy Bentham. He wrote *Offences Against One's Self: Paederasty* in 1785, promoting liberalization of anti-homosexual laws. He considered sex between consenting males a private matter. However, out of concern for public reaction to his book, it was not published in his lifetime. (5)

In colonial America, homosexuality could be punished by death. This included women in the New Haven Colony of 1655. (6) The military was no place for homosexual men. In 1778, a soldier in General George Washington's Continental Army was convicted of sodomy. "His Excellency the Commander in Chief, with abhorrence and detestation of such infamous crimes, orders the lieutenant to be drummed out of camp the following morning." (7)

Nor was the English military comforting. Four seamen were hanged for "buggery" in 1815. (8)

Twentieth century America continued to disadvantage homosexuals medically and legally. Immigration to the US was barred because they had a "psychopathic personality" and were afflicted with a mental illness. (9) Discrimination in employment was legal. In the Federal Government homosexual applicants were disqualified along with "other sex perverts". They were deemed a security risk. They were vulnerable to blackmail because of the public and legal condemnation of their sexuality. (10)

Frank Kameny worked for the state department Army Map Service with his doctorate in astronomy from Harvard. In 1957, he was exposed as homosexual and fired. This experience launched a national leader in gay rights. He was the first openly homosexual candidate for US Congress in 1971. He lost. (11) In 1974, Kameny was my advocate in a television debate where I supported same-sex marriage (Section 8).

The American Law Institute promotes modernization of law and recommended decriminalization of homosexual conduct in 1955. However, a quarter of a century later the majority of US states continued to criminalize. (12) Punishment could be harsh. A ten-year prison sentence for sodomy was upheld by the Missouri Supreme Court in 1972. (13)

In England decriminalization moved more quickly than in the US. I was a spectator in the House of Commons in 1966 when the bill was endorsed that would legalize consenting sex between adult males, providing they were not in the military. Opponents of the legalization warned that it would blacken Britain's reputation abroad and provide further evidence of Britain's degeneracy. Appropriately, passage of the bill was reported in the *New York Times* on July 4, Independence Day. (14). However, not all police action against the gay population ceased. There were police stakeouts in parks and toilets. Gay saunas were raided. "Gross Indecency" convictions trebled from 1966 to 1974. (15)

In England, female homosexuality had not been illegal. Allegedly, Queen Victoria declared in 1885 that women "do not do such things".

It may be difficult for anyone under forty to empathize with what it was like then to be gay and usually closeted. Quiet discomfort began to boil. The Stonewall rebellion was the iconic event that celebrated the breakout in the US. Police harassment of patrons in a 1969 New York gay bar erupted into fight-back and riot. A colorful account was published in the *New York Daily News*: "Homo Nest Raided, Queen Bees Are Stinging Mad."(16) The first Gay Liberation Day march was a year later. (17)

With US legal reform proceeding on the shell of a snail, a swifter vehicle could be powered by mental health reform.

Sigmund Freud's 1935 nearly non-judgemental view of homosexuality in his letter to the mother of an American homosexual was but a footnote, largely ignored. His letter was in reply to hers expressing concern for her son. Although Freud did not celebrate the prospect of a homosexual child, he wrote, "We do not consider it an illness, but rather an arrest of development. By asking me if I can help, you mean, I suppose, if I can abolish homosexuality and make normal heterosexuality take its place. The answer is, in a general way, we cannot promise to achieve it. What analysis can do for your son runs in a different line. If he is unhappy, neurotic, torn by conflict, inhibited in his social life, the analysis may bring him harmony, peace of mind, full efficiency whether he remains a homosexual or gets changed." (18)

Perhaps he was influenced by his daughter Anna, his youngest child, and only psychoanalytic "heir", becoming a prominent analyst in her own right. She lived with her companion, Dorothy Burlingham, for decades. Post-Freudians were less generous in their view of homosexuality.

THREE

OUT OF BROOKLYN

Before enrolling as a student at Johns Hopkins Medical School in 1957 (under their maximum 10% Jewish quota) I took a fling at acting. A university friend told me about a summer theater acting group he was in and asked if I were interested. To my shock, at that eight-week playhouse, I was the only heterosexual male. This, it turned out, included my friend with whom I had double dated co-eds. Even the local theater critic, married with kids, was having sex with the actors. I had never knowingly known a homosexual before this.

That fall, at Hopkins, I already knew I wanted to be a psychiatrist. My psychology readings and my curiosities about my own weaknesses were strong. And, some truth to the quip: a psychiatrist is a Jewish doctor who can't stand the sight of blood. This was reinforced by the ghastly dissection of a human body in the first year gross anatomy course. Emphasis on "gross".

Hopkins had a research program for students where we had an elective semester. At the completion of a daily dissection, and reeking from formaldehyde, I climbed the stairs in the vintage psychiatric building to be interviewed by the program head. He asked, "Do you have any research experience?" The only paper I had written was in anatomy and because the genitalia were always my favorite body part, I had chosen "hermaphrodism" (where there was a mix of male and female). He informed me that he and a colleague had just completed a study on the psychology of hermaphrodites, and whether they identified as male or female. I was sent to that colleague.

John Money was in his 30s. Over several decades, he became the "Dean of American Sexology", promoting transsexual surgery, hormonal treatment of sex offenders, and unique theories of the development of gender and the many variants of sexuality.

I told John of my summer theater experience and my curiosity about how some people became homosexual. I did not know that he was bisexual. In his exotic New Zealand accent he told me that during the hermaphrodite studies a young boy had been referred because he was thought to be hermaphroditic. The boy was very feminine in play and wanted to dress as a girl. But, he was not hermaphroditic. His anatomy was conventionally male. John said he was a "psychic hermaphrodite". Today, the boy would be described as transgendered. John offered to have me sit in on the next appointment with the family. That launched my career.

Over the next three years, I interviewed eleven boys and their parents. The boys preferred girls' activities. They wanted to dress in girls' clothes. All their playmates were girls. John and I published two papers on young "psychic hermaphrodites" in 1960 and 1961 (where John graciously let me be first author). With his penchant for convoluted language, he labelled the boys as manifesting "incongruous gender role with non-genital manifestations". (1,2)

After med school I went back to Brooklyn where I'd grown up in a rent-controlled mini-apartment with no air-conditioning in the summer and malfunctioning radiators in the winter. Medical internship for a year was at Kings County Hospital, a 3000-bed public facility in a war zone. The twenty-four hour marathon emergency room shift was still permitted, although not in the best interest of either physician or patient. Meanwhile, I was applying for psychiatry training. Two decades of sweltering, then freezing, then sweltering in the East drew me to Southern California. The University of California at Los Angeles had recently opened its med school. I would train to be a psychiatrist under a palm tree.

At the opening reception for new trainees I was greeted by the psychologist Alex Rosen: "We have been waiting for you." The other half of the "we", on vacation, was Robert Stoller. I knew nothing of him. But he was the only other psychiatric researcher in the US focussed on gender identity. They had read my papers with John. They had identified a new young colleague. Bob Stoller became my mentor as

I became a member of his Gender Identity Clinic. That sealed my career.

At the Clinic I saw my first transsexual patients. Most had been born male and insisted that since early childhood they had felt female. They were desperate. But UCLA was not performing their urgently demanded surgery. They were psychological study patients only. That was unjust.

Two years later, when I was sidestepping military combat during the Vietnam War by doing research at the National Institute of Mental Health, John Money introduced me to Harry Benjamin. Harry was emerging as the "Father of Transsexualism". Since the 1950s he was treating transsexuals when no American medical facilities were available. Few physicians had heard about transsexuals. If they had, their impression was that these people were mentally ill and required psychiatric treatment, not hormonal or surgical.

Harry allowed me to sit in on his New York Saturday office hours. Some patients needed psychiatric referral to surgeons. None were available in the US. In a move that could have derailed my career (considering the negative American medical view of transsexuals at the time) I wrote letters to overseas surgeons recommending "sex-change surgery".

After returning to UCLA, I was eager to put into practice my experience with Harry. At the Gender Identity Clinic I looked for an ideal patient to convince UCLA to perform their first "sex-change". As described in Section 19, I found that person in 1969.

I include this digression because my thinking about homosexuality, and my controversial early career stand against its designation as mental illness, followed in the wake of this controversial treatment approach to the transsexual.

I also had a new friend. His name was Martin Hoffman. He was an openly gay psychiatrist living in San Francisco. He lamented that he resembled Wally Cox ("Mr Peepers" on American 1950s TV), an unattractive, balding, owlish comic who was, oddly, the closest friend of Marlon Brando.

He was "Uncle Martin" to the three young girls living with me and their mother. He stayed with us when in Los Angeles. Martin cruised "twinks", late adolescent males named after the junk food. He recounted tales of occasional conquest and frequent failure.

Martin was depressed. Ironic, then, that his book was titled *The Gay World*. (3) When I reviewed it for the *San Francisco Chronicle / Examiner,* the review title was "Somber Shades in the Gay World". My opening reference was to the sadness of the gay world. I stressed the paradox between the book's title and the painful sadness never stated but always felt in Martin's portrait of that world. His world.

Martin had his emotional problems, but it was not his sexual orientation that was his downfall and led to early death. He would not have been a roaring heterosexual success either, resembling as he did Wally Cox. And, he lamented that he was born in the wrong country and in the wrong century. At my Los Angeles poolside, he would say he should have been born in the 19th in England so he could have occupied a college room at Oxford or Cambridge. There he would have been supported for what he did best—creative thinking and scholarship. But mid-20th century psychiatry neglected his talents. Psychiatry was all about treating schizophrenia with new wonder drugs. And, an attempt by two professors, Stoller and myself, to obtain an academic appointment for Martin at UCLA was frustrated by a Department that "did not want a homosexual" on its faculty.

At poolside, I would sip California Burgundy and write while Martin would swallow pills and share his feelings of despair. In his obituary, I wrote, "I do not know whether the pills that brought Martin to a dead halt were to ease the pain in his head, or in his psyche. It does not matter. The loss for us and the peace to him are the same." (4)

With Martin, I met a lot of homosexual men, more commonly being referred in the 1960s as "gay". Many were three-piece suited lawyers, doctors, accountants. What was the problem here? Unless one observed them in a sexual moment, these people seemed like every other lawyer, doctor, accountant. Wanting to have sex with a man wasn't that unusual. Many millions did. Because most of them were women did not seem relevant to control by others. This was not sex with five-year olds, or siblings, or the pet dog. If a religion or two or three considered it to be a sin, that should not set national policy. If many people considered it to be immoral, it did not follow that it was mental illness.

FOUR

RATTLING PSYCHIATRY'S CAGE

Psychiatry's equation "Homosexuality=Mental Illness" required challenge. In 1972, writing for a psychiatry journal, I assaulted the orthodox position from several perspectives: biology, sociology, the theory of homosexual development, the mental health of homosexual and heterosexual patients, and the role of psychiatry in the larger society. (1) I was convinced: homosexuality did not make a person mentally ill, the psychiatry manual of mental disorders did.

Biology

Heterosexuality, required for human reproduction and survival, was a bedrock argument for homosexuality being awry. But, if there was an evolutionary advantage for innate heterosexuality, this should not be an absolute criterion by which to judge homosexual behavior. If heterosexuality is indispensible to ensure species survival, and universal homosexuality catastrophic, must homosexual behavior by many people some of the time or a few people all of the time be biologically hazardous? Must it be mental illness?

If heterosexuality is inborn, could homosexuality also be inborn? Reports at the time of twin studies where both twins were homosexual lent support. If further research revealed that hormonal variations or genes caused homosexuality, rather than early life pathogenic family relationships, this would have a profound effect on psychiatric theory.

Theory of Homosexual Development

Based on experience with homosexuals who sought help, psychiatrists concluded that homosexuality was a mental illness. The gold standard psychoanalytic doctrine of the time branded an unresolved Oedipal family romance and castration fear as promoting a same-sex erotic attraction. But the supporting evidence came from patients who were maladaptive to the extent of seeking extended, expensive psychiatric treatment. It was reported by clinicians who ascribed to this psychological theory and interpreted patient behavior in that light.

Sociology

Being sexually at odds with the great majority of society was interpreted as another sign of mental illness. But difficulties in defining "normality" in sexual behavior was poignantly demonstrated in the extensive sexual history reporting by Kinsey of thousands in the 1950s. Consider "male mouth-female breast" contact during sex play by married couples. This was quite "normal" for those with at least thirteen years of education (four in five) but "abnormal" for those with fewer than eight years (one in three). (2)

Moreover, homosexual behavior was not disparaged across all cultures. In a survey of seventy-six societies, two-thirds considered homosexuality of one sort or another to be normal or socially acceptable for some members of the community. (3)

Mental Health of Patients

Psychiatrists saw patients not coping well with many aspects of their life. Additionally, for the homosexual, coping was aggravated by secrecy and discrimination.

I argued that a review of my heterosexual patients' experiences might conclude that heterosexuality is a condition of seeking emotional and sexual gratification in a relationship between two persons of a different sex that is associated with anxiety, depression, and unfulfilled dependency needs.

Supporters of the Homosexuality=Mental Illness equation stressed the promiscuity and instability of relationships in the male homosexual world. I argued that, rather than it being an indicator of the inability of homosexual couples to establish meaningful relationships, it could be a consequence of the extraordinary societal pressure working against such a union.

The Role of Psychiatry

Psychiatry had a responsibility to the wider culture and to influence societal values. It was a respected profession. I agreed with the "Gay Liberation" position that with homosexuality psychiatry should be more concerned with "treating" public values than an individual's behavior. It was placing a higher value on the heterosexual one-night stand than on the homosexual liaison of six-months duration. I called for a psychiatric diagnosis for the "quality" of sexuality, and not its direction.

In my paper, I decided to reveal my sexual orientation as heterosexual. "It can be argued that a homosexual psychiatrist would invoke special pleading in defense of his own defect." I challenged other heterosexual psychiatrists: "I suppose it is a comfort to feel we have matured well in our psychosexuality. Perhaps we experience a measured sense of competence and comfort when we find evidence of defect or illness in others which merit our treatment."

Few gay psychiatrists were "out" in 1972. I asked, "What would be the impact on psychiatry if all homosexual psychiatrists in America were to openly acknowledge their sexual preference? If the per cent is comparable to the general population, there are some eight hundred exclusively homosexual psychiatrists."

What I wrote next was prescient: "Consider an American Psychiatric Association task force, composed of homosexual psychiatrists, preparing a report addressing the prevailing theories of the etiology of homosexuality (written, for the most part, by heterosexuals)." Ten years later, the Association set up the Caucus of Homosexually-Identified Psychiatrists.

The journal where my paper was published in 1972 invited discussants to comment. They were not uniformly congratulatory. Charles Socarides was the standard bearer for psychoanalysts relentlessly arguing that homosexuals were mentally ill.

Socarides began his tirade: "There is such a total lack of scientific veracity in the Green paper that it would hardly merit discussion by any busy and seriously committed psychiatrist. However, to prevent the damage that can be done by such a travesty of medical reporting..." (He found the time.)

My mentor, John Money, advised me not to publish this paper. "It will ruin your career. Put it into a drawer and forget about it." But, father doesn't always know best.

FIVE

THE UNUSUAL SUSPECTS

Three introductions. These psychiatrists feature prominently here.

Judd Marmor

Judd Marmor was born in London and cut a dashing figure as a Los Angeles psychoanalyst. I recall him appearing at one of our Saturday morning Gender Identity Clinic meetings in shorts, gripping his tennis racket.

Judd was a modern incarnation of psychoanalysis, giving more importance to culture and environment than the instinctual drives of classical theory—castration anxiety and Oedipal conflict. The analytic institute to which he belonged was the rival of the institute whose members included Bob Stoller and where I trained until I jumped ship and quit. Judd's institute admitted openly homosexual psychiatrists. Actually, Freud had not seen that as a barrier. (1)

Judd's vigorous campaigning to delist homosexuality as a mental illness was a headline, as he was President of the American Psychiatric Association. I took comfort in his prestige as I campaigned from the lower ranks.

We co-authored psychiatric textbook chapters arguing that homosexuality was not mental illness. When I wore my lawyer's hat, he was the first witness I examined in a courtroom. It was the "Gay Boy Scout" case (described in Section 12). We lunched together at the UCLA Faculty Club until I emigrated to the country of his birth.

Irving Bieber

Irving Bieber looked like my Brooklyn tailor. A New York psychoanalyst, he argued to retain homosexuality as a mental disorder. But he was not aggressively anti-homosexual like Charles Socarides (the next suspect). He did not pop up everywhere like a Jack-in-the-box to preach his position, or provide clinical evidence that could be used against homosexual men and women in their struggle for equal rights.

To his credit, Irving constructed a questionnaire for co-analysts who were treating homosexual men asking for descriptions of the early relationship of their patients with mother and father. He analysed the results (statistically). (2) His conclusion had the fallacy of identifying chicken and egg. Homosexual men reported a close-binding mother, and a distant, hostile father. He concluded that this caused homosexuality. But my work with cross-gender behaving boys who became homosexual men showed that the boys gravitated to their mother because they had more interests in common than with their father who expected conventionally masculine behavior. (3)

Charles Socarides

Charles Socarides was a handsome man with a theatrically resonate voice. He was the most outspoken psychiatrist proclaiming homosexuality was a mental illness that could be cured.

He was also a hypocrite. He protested that he was a staunch advocate of civil rights for homosexuals. Yet, in the legal challenge to a state constitutional amendment that limited the rights of gays and lesbians (reported in Section 14), his affidavit argued that homosexuality could be changed. This undermined our argument that it was "immutable" in legal terms, and therefore constitutionally protected. Socarides' testimony was precisely the evidence sought by supporters of the anti-gay law.

Charles was uncompromising for decades in his psychoanalytic condemnation of homosexuality as pathology. One example was his TV appearance opposing me on *The Advocates* (reported in Section 8) debating same-sex marriage in 1974.

I wondered whether Charles protested too much. He continued to demonstrate his heterosexual prowess with his fourth wife and having a fifth child at an age when most colleagues had retired from procreation.

My bias on the origins of homosexuality leans toward innate factors, with a genetic contribution. Charles' son, Richard, is gay.

I do not think that Charles was a "closet gay." But could Charles have been battling a repressed homosexual drive in his relentless battle against this in other men? Or, could his son's homosexuality be a dramatic Oedipal challenge: Take that, my mother's fucker.

SIX

PUBLIC HEALTH'S
GREATEST MOMENT

It was the greatest public health triumph ever. Four million Americans were cured of the same illness, all at the same time.

In December 1973, the American Psychiatric Association (APA) removed homosexuality from the list of mental disorders. (1) The APA press release announced, "The Trustees of the American Psychiatric Association … today ruled that 'homosexuality' shall no longer be listed as a 'mental disorder' in its official nomenclature of mental disorders. The category of homosexuality is now replaced by 'sexual orientation disturbance' for individuals whose sexual interests are directed towards people of the same sex and who are either disturbed by, in conflict with, or wish to change, their sexual orientation. This is distinguished from homosexuality, which by itself does not constitute a psychiatric disorder."

Rumblings for change were heard around the time I began writing my 1972 challenge to psychiatry arguing for its removal from the manual of disorders. A series of tumultuous psychiatric conventions dragged the APA toward change: 1970 in San Francisco, 1972 in Dallas, 1973 in Honolulu.

The 1970 meeting was anarchy. San Francisco had the greatest concentration of American gays. In the Castro district, heterosexual men could qualify as an endangered species. Demonstrators besieged the meeting. An Australian psychiatrist was shouted down while trying to read his preliminary research paper. For years he had been attempting to "cure" homosexual men with electric shocks to homosexual imagery. He pleaded with the audience for quiet in order to hear him. Ironically, a few years later the conclusion of his research was that these treatments were ineffective. (2) Another older psychiatrist was ushered off the platform by a female colleague, "Come, you will have a heart attack."

I had organized an evening panel on homosexuality featuring a biologist who researched the role of sex hormones before birth, and a clinician who treated homosexuals. With the audience bulging with gay activists, I feared a wholesale riot. To avoid pandemonium I alternated panel members with an unarmed audience member. We survived a spirited, but orderly, debate.

One impressed audience member was Seymour Weingarten, the editor at Plenum Press who had recently signed me on to edit a new journal, *Archives of Sexual Behavior.* Seymour had initially asked Robert Stoller to be editor but my mentor wisely preserved his precious time for his sex and gender research. He suggested me. I was pleased that after that evening Seymour thanked Stoller, who was not at the panel, for his choice. It was important that my surrogate father be proud.

The 1972 Dallas meeting made headlines when a psychiatrist, disguised in a bizarre mask, calling himself, "Dr. Anonymous", declared his homosexuality before an audience of co-psychiatrists. (3) His disguise received national press coverage.

Our 1973 Honolulu panel was attended by a thousand. Panel members included both psychoanalytic stalwarts of the "homosexuality is a disease" camp--Charles Socarides and Irving Bieber, and its critics--Judd Marmor, Robert Stoller and me, plus the gay activist, Ron Gold. (4)

Bieber explained: "Dislocations in heterosexual organization of biologically normal children occur as a consequence of pathological family formation. Homosexuality is not an adaptation of choice; it is brought about by fears that inhibit satisfactory heterosexual functioning."

Socarides proclaimed: "Homosexuality represents a disorder of sexual development and does not fall within the range of normal. A pathological parent-child relationship is always in the background."

Marmor countered: "All personality idiosyncrasies are the result of background developmental differences and all have specific historical antecedents. We do not have the right to label behavior that is deviant from that currently favored by the majority as evidence of psychopathology."

Stoller parked himself on middle ground: "Homosexualtiy is not a diagnosis. There is homosexual behavior. It is varied. There is no such thing as homosexuality. It is not a diagnosis because it is a sexual preference, not a constellation of signs and symptoms."

Ron Gold was sensational with the neon title of his talk: "Stop It, You're Making Me Sick!!"

The symposium listing was "Should Homosexuality be in the APA Nomenclature?" I titled my talk "Should Heterosexuality be in the APA Nomenclature?" My view was that for some people homosexuality caused difficulties. However, for others, so did heterosexuality. The manual of mental disorders was biased—the homosexual was always mentally disordered.

Four major criteria typically classified behavior as disorder. I argued that homosexuality did not meet the criteria.

"First is gross social dysfunction: the regressed schizophrenic, the manic, or the profoundly depressed. This did not describe the typical homosexual."

"Second is inner turmoil that reduces the efficiency of social function—severe anxiety and phobias. The homosexual was typically no different from the heterosexual counterpart."

DR ANONYMOUS

"Third is culturally deviant behavior. But using statistical deviance as a diagnostic basis causes problems. So, too, are vegetarians, pacifists, the celibate, and the esoterically religious."

"Then there is the softest of criteria. A theoretical model of psychological development -- classic psychoanalytic theory: castration fear, penis envy. Its scientific merits have been debated at length."

I proposed an alternative psychiatric listing. It was Amorous Relationship Disorder:

"The heterosexual or the homosexual who finds it difficult to maintain a love relationship, and who compulsively uses sexuality to ward off anxiety or depression or as a substitute for feelings of self-worth."

This became an argument in my later running gun battle with Robert Spitzer over what, if anything, should remain of homosexuality in the revised list of disorders.

Spitzer headed the committee for revising the list of psychiatric disorders and organized and chaired our panel. He was slowly being won over by some psychiatrists and gay activists and moved in evolutionary steps to join our revolution. With his newly formulated criteria for disorder as subjective distress and social disadvantage, he acknowledged that not all people who were homosexual fit. He favored a new entry for homosexuals distressed over their sexual orientation. This was "sexual orientation disturbance". (Abbreviated, this was SOD, as in sodomy!)

(Although we were frequently embattled, as shown later in our correspondence, I had to admire Bob one day in Central Park in New York. There he was playing the banjo with his son. At their feet was a hat to collect coins from grateful passers-by. How could you not admire someone like that? The musically adept Woody Allen of psychiatry.)

When homosexuality was deleted from the list of disorders, the shit hit the psychoanalytic fan. Analysts flailed at their couches. Socarides, Bieber, and other frantics instituted a referendum to be voted on by the full psychiatric membership on whether to uphold the Board of Trustees decision.

In response, I wrote to the APA *Psychiatric News*: "What kind of medical science decides issues of fact with public opinion polling? Psychiatry has been ridiculed as a non-science by the rest of medicine and other academic disciplines. The referendum placed before the APA membership deciding whether homosexuality is a mental disorder makes a mockery of psychiatry, and flaunts this mockery in full public view."

With 10,000 voting, the decision was upheld by nearly sixty per cent. (1) This was science's finest outing, cross-dressed as democracy. Years later, the International Astronomical Union tried but failed to match that pinnacle when it voted to delete Pluto as a planet. (5)

Psychoanalytic writers were furious. Stanley Lesse wrote, "The recent pronouncement by the APA Board of Trustees is not binding upon serious, thinking psychiatrists, psychotherapists, and social scientists who find its viewpoint an illogical step backward into clinical confusion and denial." (6) Decades later, Socarides remained furious. "To declare a condition a 'non-condition' a group of practitioners had it removed from our list of serious psychosexual disorders. It involved an out-of-hand and peremptory disregard and dismissal of hundreds of psychiatric and psychoanalytic research papers. This action remains a chilling reminder that if scientific principles are not fought for, they can be lost." (7)

Our battle was won, but the war continued. Homosexuality, in some circumstances, could still be diagnosed in the manual of disorders using other labels. "A skunk by any other name…"

The *Diagnostic and Statistical Manual of Mental Disorders, Version III (DSM-III)* was in the making. I was on the committee formulating sex and gender diagnoses. I insisted that homosexuality be erased in all forms. Judd Marmor agreed, although not a committee member, as did Kent Robinson, a prominent psychiatrist in Maryland, also not a member.

I wrote to Judd in March 1977, "I totally agree with you that psychiatric nomenclatures that still seek to include homosexuality in a special diagnostic slot are archaic. I agree that if a homosexual is distressed about his orientation, the appropriate diagnosis should be the underlying psychological disorder, such as anxiety reaction, depressive reaction."

In April 1977 I wrote to committee members, "I request your support in going on record so as to exclude homosexuality, be it called dyshomophilia, recently suggested by Spitzer, or sexual orientation disturbance, from *DSM-III,* when it can be listed under anxiety reaction, depressive reaction, or some other category. Or, if dyshomophilia is be included, it should have as its parallel dysheterophilia for those who would prefer more comfort in relating in a homosexual situation." Although I recognized that this patient group would not be substantial, it would help reduce the stigma attached to homosexuality.

Richard Pillard was one of the first openly gay psychiatrists in academia. He and I were awarded a Research Scientist Development Award by the National Institute of Mental Health early in our careers. Though he was not a committee member, I wrote to him in May 1977: "This is to bring you up-to-date on what I've been doing with respect to 'dyshomophilia'. The first concession Spitzer is making is to possibly remove it from the paraphilias, psychiatry's less offensive new label for "perversions". It would be sandwiched between exhibitionism and pedophilia (hardly an advance in either scientism or judgementalism)."

"What I plan to do now: I will poll each member of the three committees involved with terminology in the area of human sexuality. Do they wish any form of homosexuality (by whatever name it is called) to remain? If unsuccessful, we should go to the Task Force on Nomenclature. If unsuccessful again in having homosexuality removed entirely except perhaps as a subordinate classification, we go to the Committee on Research."

In writing this, Winston Churchill came to mind: "We shall fight them on the beaches, we shall fight them in the streets…we shall never surrender."

The poll options of June 1977:

"Sexual orientation disorder and/or dyshomophilia should be eliminated as a diagnostic entity. Any issue including homosexuality should be listed under "Psychosexual Disorders Not Elsewhere Classified".

"Or, it should be listed under depression if this is the primary mental state, or anxiety, secondary to discomfort over homosexual (or same sex) arousal pattern."

"Or, it should remain as conflict with sexual orientation, but with two subtypes: homosexual and heterosexual."

"Or, it should remain within the paraphilias."

The consensus from my poll was that it could be placed under the miscellaneous category, "Psychosexual Disorders Not Elsewhere Classified".

Kent Robinson astutely pointed out to the committee that Spitzer was labelling a conflict rather than a specific condition. "Nowhere in *DSM-III* is the conflict labelled as the diagnosis. Certainly, there are people in conflict about their sexual orientation, just as there are many other people who consult us who are in conflict about all kinds of things."

Then Spitzer proposed "ego-dystonic homosexuality" for homosexual patients in conflict about their sexuality. When I had proposed a diagnosis for heterosexual patients who wanted to experience homosexual arousal his objection was incoherent. He stated that it could not be included because "a wish to increase one's sexual responsiveness does not meet the criteria for a mental disorder". I countered, "Will all of your 'ego-dystonic homosexuals' want to eliminate homosexuality or will many want to add heterosexuality?"

I told Spitzer that a diagnosis similar to what he had heard me propose in Honolulu in 1973 was being considered by our committee. It was "Amorous Relationship Disorder for those persons who experience repeated difficulty maintaining stable romantic relationships." These were patients with whom most psychiatrists spend most of their time.

Victory was delayed.

DSM-III came into effect in 1980. It contained "ego-dystonic homosexuality". (8) At a meeting commemorating the tenth anniversary of the 1973 decision held at New York Medical College, Judd Marmor and I "deplored the continued listing of distress about one's homosexuality as an illness as it fosters continuing prejudice and discrimination." (9)

DSM-III R (Revised) appeared in 1987. (10) Just prior to its release, word spread that "ego-dystonic homosexuality" was finally gone. I wrote to *Psychiatric News,* recalling that "The decision to include ego-dystonic homosexuality was a political compromise, there being the fear that the whole question of homosexuality as a mental disorder per se would be reopened. The scientific data then are not different from those now. Homosexuals did not, and do not, satisfy the DSM criteria of mental disorder. Today, however, the political gains made by American homosexuals, including psychiatrists, have taken a firmer hold. So now ego-dystonic homosexuality disappears into the well-deserved abyss of the black hole of dead diagnoses." (11)

The corpse of homosexuality was interred as "sexual disorder not otherwise specified". We had suggested this diagnosis a decade earlier.

SEVEN

FAMILY COURT: LESBIAN/ GAY PARENTS

When I was to be the first psychiatric witness in a lesbian-mother child custody trial in 1974 in Ohio, colleagues asked, "Where in Ohio?" When I replied, "Licking County", they thought this was a pun in poor taste.

(The case: Hall v Hall, Ohio Court of Domestic Relations, Licking County, October 31, 1974.)

Earlier cases had not gone well for lesbian mothers. In 1947, an Ohio court would only allow the mother to retain custody if her female partner left the home. (1) In 1959, a California court awarded custody to the father in consequence of the "moral character, conduct and disposition" of the mother. (2) In another California case, the court made an ironic ruling in granting custody to the lesbian mother's mother. She had also raised a gay son. (3)

After a couple of days interviewing Mrs. Hall, her female partner, and her daughter, my courtroom testimony covered many topics. They followed questions from the mother's attorney.

Is this lesbian mother emotionally stable? Can she commit to a relationship?

"She is stable, being committed to the people with whom she has been involved romantically. She was married twice to the same individual in an effort to continue that relationship. She has currently been involved in a romantic and sexual relationship for three years, which indicates stability, a sign of maturation and sexual health."

Will the child witness lesbian lovemaking?

"Both she and her partner are careful in not exposing the girl to explicit sex acts. What might be available could be common kinds of affection, perhaps an occasional hug or kiss."

Does this woman hate men?

"She gets along better with men in terms of a working relationship...it is with respect to the sexual part of her life that women are preferred, but her feelings toward men are not at all hostile, but in fact quite warm and positive."

Will this couple try to raise a masculine daughter?

"They adhere to rather traditional stereotypic ways of what is considered "appropriately" fem-

inine and "appropriately" masculine. The toys available are primarily Barbie dolls. With respect to clothing, dresses are primarily provided. It is a very pro-female identity and pro-feminine kind of child-raising that she is having."

Is the mother's partner emotionally stable and capable of a long-term relationship?

"She was first engaged in a homosexual relationship at eighteen which lasted for five years. A second was for ten years, and then the current for three."

Is the young daughter developing as a "normal" girl?

"She has a sexual identity of being female. She is a feminine little girl. She says she has not one, but two boyfriends. One of them in particular she would like to marry."

What causes a homosexual orientation?

"There are a number of theories. They can be divided into inborn and social learning. Probably the most sober view today is that there is an interaction."

Will living with a lesbian mother promote lesbianism in the daughter?

"It is erroneous to say that because the parents are homosexual the children will be. Almost all homosexuals have had heterosexual mothers and fathers."

If not developing as a lesbian, what will be the effect on the daughter?

"The most significant effect would be that the child would tend to view homosexuality in others in a more tolerant and less prejudiced manner than the child who grows up with the typical kind of myths they may get from street corner gossip."

Is homosexuality a mental disorder?

"The American Psychiatric Association has recently concluded that homosexuality in itself is not a sign of mental illness or emotional disorder."

Will the child be stigmatized by peers knowing that her mother is a lesbian?

"We are going through a period of dramatic social change. I don't believe the child is going to be stigmatized more than all children who, for a variety of reasons, are teased, for example, because they are short or tall, fat or skinny, or not good athletes. Weighing the possible embarrassment she may experience against continuing in a solid home relationship, I come out on the side of continuing the home relationship."

After a lengthy testimony, summarized above, the first question from the judge:

"DR. GREEN, HOW IS THE SEX ACT BETWEEN LESBIANS ACCOMPLISHED?"

His education complete, the judge awarded child custody to the mother. The testimony transcript became the early reference for attorneys representing mothers in similar cases.

Another court however, where I was a psychiatric witness, took a very dim view of a mother's homosexuality. If she had "abandoned the practice of lesbianism", the court "might have been tempted to experiment". But she would not. In an uniquely "bacteriologic" concern about female homosexuality, the judge pronounced, "I am struck by the primacy that lesbians give to multiple **organisms** (sic)". (4) Beware an epidemic.

Again, the case was school for a trial court judge of just what lesbians were up to sexually. He asked, "How do you do it?" The appeals court held that there was no trial judge error in "compelling the mother to answer questions about the intimate details of her sex life." This because "the trial court did not know precisely what occurred. It was appropriate for the court to receive a primer education in the sexual techniques of lesbians." (5)

A much-publicized case in 1974 where I was a witness involved the consolidated custody battles of two families. This couple and sets of children were living as a combined family. They had appeared on television, and made a film featuring the famed anthropologist Margaret Mead. (6)

The trial lasted six days. There were thirty-three witnesses. The mothers were "damned with faint praise" by the judge: "They have shown stability, integrity, and openness, despite their homosexuality." I testified, as did others, that the children were "healthy, happy, normal, loving children". The mothers retained custody but were required to live apart. (7) The judge cautioned: "I don't think this case should be regarded as any landmark. The decision is not any stamp of approval by the Court on homosexuality." Then, with a touch of understatement, "It is a case just like cases that we decide every day."

Testifying for lesbian mothers who were fit parents was not without personal conflict. Child custody courts were not an even playing field in conventional heterosexual divorce cases. Fathers were typically on the steep downhill end. But while this inequity required challenge, I did not view a mother's sexual orientation as the weapon of choice.

Before agreeing to assess the mother and children, she and her attorney understood that after my assessment I might not testify favorably. While I did not believe that being a homosexual parent disqualifies one as a fit parent, my clinical conclusion might be that the mother should not have custody. Sometimes, the attorney would prepare a document saying that my testimony might not be in her client's favor.

In some trials, I presented results of our research on the development of children with a parent living as homosexual after divorce. We had evaluated twenty-one children living in two-adult-female families. "The evidence does not show any significant negative influence. The children do not show conflict with respect to their own sexuality. They are developing as typical male and female children. They look like most other kids." (9)

Statements by a child could be helpful in court. A twelve-year-old boy told me that people should have the right to live the way they want to live with a person of the same sex. "That's fine with me. It is not something I would like to do. There is nothing wrong, but I wouldn't want to live with another man, myself."

Along with my mentor, John Money, I testified in a case arguing for joint child custody by a gay father. The father was a scientist at a New York research center. The mother was a physician. Father was also the Director of the National Gay Task Force. The principal court concern was the involvement of the children in gay rights demonstrations. The mother contended that the father's "total involvement with and dedication to furthering homosexuality has created an environment, exposure to which in anything more than a minimal amount would be harmful." The children had accompanied him on protest marches, at rallies, and were filmed with him for a television show.

The expert witness for the mother, a child psychoanalyst, opined that "the total environment could impede healthy sexual development. The father's milieu could engender homosexual fantasies causing confusion and anxiety. It is possible that these children upon reaching puberty would be subject to either overt or covert homosexual seduction."

We lost. The court ordered that "during child visitation, the father was not to be in the presence of his lover. He was not to involve the children in any homosexually-oriented activities or publicity." (8)

There was another personal conflict in my testimony. Assurances were often given to the court that the likelihood of the children becoming homosexual was not increased by living with a homosexual parent. The inference was that this would be an unwanted effect. Although I did not accept this potential outcome as negative, for the time and the political climate, this assurance was required.

I reported an interview where a mother told me that she wouldn't specifically object if one of the children turned out to be gay, but she knew the difficulties of being gay and so would prefer that the children not be. I had asked her if she wanted her child to be gay, how she would go about that. Of course, she didn't know the answer. I added for the court: "Neither does anybody else." (9)

Concerns over the sexual orientation of a parent in child custody disputes may not be as passé as might be expected four decades after these cases. A 2014 article published in a journal of the American Psychological Association is titled: "Lesbian and Gay Parents and Determination of Child Custody: The Changing Legal Landscape and Implications for Policy and Practice." (10)

EIGHT

SAME-SEX MARRIAGE

The US Public Broadcasting System series *The Advocates* broadcast my clash with anti-gay psychiatrist Charles Socarides. Gay activist Frank Kameny was my supporting advocate. The subject for debate was same-sex marriage. It was May 2, 1974. (1) Over 90% of Americans opposed same-sex marriage. (2)

The show was recorded at the campus of the University of California at Irvine with many students in attendance. Frank set out his stall with the lament that "even the right to have rights is frequently not recognized." Then, "for society to accuse us of unstable, short-term relationships and then to deny us a powerful means of stabilization is to make their accusation self-fulfilling in a peculiarly vicious way."

Frank asked me whether homosexuality was a sickness. I replied:

"That is an outmoded, outdated bias based on a lack of scientific information, based on biased

clinical experience that most of us who are psychiatrists have had".

I emphasized the non-representativeness of people we see for psychiatric issues:

"Most of us as psychiatrists have seen people troubled by their sexuality and have generalized from that to the entire population of people that we do not see."

I added scientific clout:

"This has been challenged during the last five to six years... there are studies, over one thousand persons, male and female, heterosexual and homosexual, who were not patients...there is no difference on any dimension of mental health. This research has been translated into recent action by the American Psychiatric Association that has deleted homosexuality in itself as a mental illness from the list of psychiatric disorders."

Frank asked how legal marriage would affect the mental health of homosexuals. The answer was lofty, but true:

"...the greatest single event and the greatest single signal that we have as adults is our ability to share with another human being, to commit ourselves to an enduring, loving relationship. In our society marriage is that social signal which says to the world that we have reached that level of matu-

ration, that we can go through life in a meaningful, enduring interpersonal relationship."

Back to Frank's earlier lament:

"Those of us who look upon the instability of homosexual relationships, and at the same time deny them the same kinds of social support systems that heterosexuals have, are using a circular logic. The capacity for maturation and growth in our society is best signified by marriage, but to deny the homosexual the right to marry does not permit that person the same opportunities for mental growth."

The impact on young people was Frank's next plank. "How would legalization of homosexual marriage help young people, teenagers?"

"Most adolescents when they discover their homosexuality are shocked and terrified because they have no one to turn to. They feel stigmatized and alienated in a heterosexual world. Our primary responsibility to those who consult us is to reassure, so long as they are not harming other people, that it is their wishes and their lifestyle that is important. If there were available for these teenagers same-sex models where they can see the same kinds of happiness, their mental health is going to be enhanced, their anxiety, alienation, and depression is going to be reduced."

The advocate for the opposition took his opportunity to challenge me:

"Doesn't society have a duty to encourage heterosexual potential of our youth? Wouldn't you, as counsellor, help a patient to realize his heterosexual rather than his homosexual potential?"

I countered: **"Society's major commitment ought to be for the most self-actualization of any individual. There are happy heterosexuals, there are unhappy ones, happy homosexuals, unhappy ones."**

Then, my opponent's zinger: "Isn't it a fact that the concept of a legal marriage for the homosexual is nothing more than an excuse for certain tax and property advantages?"

My response: **"I have more respect for marriage than merely as a tax shelter. I don't think it's like drilling for oil wells."** (From the student audience: loud laughter.)

Next the advocate's "SSS" ploy, the silly slippery slope: "Since homosexual marriage will not produce children should they be subject to the laws against incest? Why can't homosexual brothers marry? Or fathers and sons? Or mothers and daughters?"

On this slippery slope was a squish of apples and pears: **"Incest can be heterosexual or homosexual. It is sexual victimization that has nothing to do with a marital issue. And if you are concerned about reproduction in marriage, why not**

limit marriage to those heterosexuals who wish to reproduce?"

Charles Socarides had his turn. He was asked by his advocate to describe the homosexual. It was his usual uncompromising depiction:

"The homosexual is a product of a process of very, very bad child rearing practices which make him on many occasions have an equilibrium which is quite unstable…the homosexual act itself is an exquisitely designed system which helps keep him in equilibrium."

Charles was asked whether "legalizing the homosexual union would aid the homosexual or add to his instability".

He warned: "The bonds might cause considerable anxiety. Most homosexuals must seek numerous parties in order to try and find themselves, the replicas of themselves." He took no prisoners. "Marriage would be social recklessness. A psychiatric disaster has already happened in trying to normalize homosexuality. A man must be a man, a woman must be a woman. The effect of this (normalization) on society will be enormous. Adolescents will be put into despair because medicine and psychiatry is now saying 'There is nothing wrong with you'."

That was 1974.

When William Rehnquist was Chief Justice of the US Supreme Court and visited Yale Law School in 1986, when I was a second year student, I asked him to speculate on a hypothetical same-sex marriage case. In the event that a state was to permit it, and there was a challenge, would the Supreme Court hear the case? He replied that he could not think of a federal constitutional question that would be involved, and so the Court would not take the case.

The speed with which same-sex marriage was legally accepted in the US was hardly breath-taking. It continued to be denied in all states for nearly two decades after the television debate until Massachusetts broke ranks. But if a couple married in Massachusetts would their marital status be recognized in another state? Marriage is usually recognized across states under the Full Faith and Credit clause of the Constitution. (3) But some states were balking.

In 1996, President Clinton signed the Defense of Marriage Act (DOMA). (4) It made male-female marriage the only union recognized under federal law. This got the objecting states off the hook for recognizing same-sex marriage across state lines.

DOMA was challenged at the Supreme Court. They did take the case. The Court ruled that defining marriage as only between a male and a female violated due process and equal protection as guaranteed in the Constitution. Justice Kennedy wrote that the law had "no legitimate purpose and disparages and injures those whom the state marriage laws sought to protect in their personhood." (5)

That was nearly four decades after *The Advocates*.

THE ADVOCATES: 1974

GIVE ME YOUR TIRED, YOUR POOR, YOUR HUDDLED (HETEROSEXUAL) MASSES YEARNING TO BREATHE FREE

The inscription at the Statue of Liberty in New York harbor welcoming immigrants to America was incomplete.

Homosexuals were first excluded from the US by the Immigration Act of 1917. It prohibited entry of "persons of constitutional psychopathic inferiority", as certified by a physician. These unwanted persons were said to show "a lifelong and constitutional tendency not to conform to the customs of the group." They would "habitually misbehave and have no sense of responsibility to their fellow men." (1,2) The 1918 Public Health Service Manual on Examination of

Aliens characterized constitutional psychopathic inferiority as a "borderland between sanity and insanity". It included "moral imbeciles, pathological liars, swindlers" and those with "abnormal sexual instincts". (3)

In 1947 the US Congress substituted "psychopathic personality" for "constitutional psychopathic inferiority"-- perhaps a bit less pejorative. In 1950, the Senate considered enlarging the class to specifically include "homosexuals and other sex perverts". However, express reference to "homosexuals or sex perverts" was deleted because the Public Health Service advised that excluding those with psychopathic personality was adequate. (4)

Difficulty in diagnosing a homosexual in an interview was acknowledged by the Immigration and Naturalization Service (INS). "In some instances where the action and behavior is obvious, as might be in transvestism or fetishism, the condition may be easily substantiated." If an alien made an "unsolicited unambiguous admission of homosexuality or was identified as a homosexual by another party arriving in the US at the same time", the alien would be barred. (5) The following guidance was ominous: "While ordinarily a history of homosexuality must be obtained from the individual, he may cover up. Some psychological tests may be helpful in uncovering homosexuality of which the individual himself may be unaware." (6)

After the American Psychiatric Association decided that homosexuality was no longer a mental illness in 1973, the INS required a new strategy to exclude the homosexual. The term "psychopathic personality" became a "legal term of art" for the government, not a medical diagnosis. It was what the government declared it to be for its purposes. (7)

Chester Morales had been admitted from Nicaragua to the US in 1962. A decade later, the INS charged that at the time of his admission he "was afflicted with a psychopathic personality, sexual deviation, homosexuality". Morales was ordered to appear before the INS to challenge his deportation.

I was requested by Lambda Legal and Educational Fund, the gay rights group, to prepare an affidavit to be submitted to the government on his behalf. It was to address the issue of whether a homosexual is a "psychopathic personality" or has a "sexual deviation".

I described psychiatry's view of homosexuality over the decades as background for Morales' argument. Psychiatry's first list of disorders, the *Diagnostic and Statistical Manual I*, published in 1952, included "psychopathic personality" along with "sexual deviation". In its second list, published in 1968, the diagnosis became "sociopathic personality disturbance". These people were considered to be ill "primarily in terms of society and of conformity with the prevailing cultural milieu." "Sexual deviations" included homosexuality, pedophilia, and sexual sadism (including rape, sexual assault, and mutilation). Deviant sexual behaviors included those "directed primarily toward objects other than people of the opposite sex; toward sexual acts not usually associated with intercourse, or toward intercourse with dead people or children."

But, from 1973, homosexuality was no longer a mental illness.

To provide a contrast with Morales who had lived successfully in the US, I described the prevailing psychiatric picture of psychopathic or sociopathic individuals: they show no regard for the general morals or principles of the larger society, repeatedly victimize others without feelings of guilt, fail to learn from experience, and are incapable of forming deep, lasting relationships.

My *curriculum vitae* (CV) and the affidavit were submitted to the government. The government agreed that my CV (termed "life picture") qualified me as an expert in human sexuality, homosexuality, and general psychiatry. My affidavit was entered into the record.

At the hearing, Morales admitted to his statement affirming his homosexuality at the time of his entry, but denied that he had been afflicted with a psychopathic personality. He argued that homosexuality was not a psychopathic personality because it was inconsistent with the clinical description as stated in my affidavit.

Through his attorney, Morales contended that the INS classification of homosexuality was arbitrary and capricious because it lacked support in scientific and medical research, again as stated in my affidavit. Therefore, the attorney argued, it was a violation of due process guaranteed by the US Constitution.

Morales had spent the previous decade in the US where he worked and studied. His attorney argued,

"Now, for no apparent reason, after all of the years of quiet enjoyment of the benefits of residence in the US, and what any reasonable person in similar circumstances would regard as a justifiable expectation that he would be allowed to remain in the US, he had suddenly received a Notice of Hearing for Deportation." In a branch of law known as equity, there is a defense of "laches"(fairness, due to duration and circumstance). In this case, the government, having done nothing to deport Morales in all those years, should be stopped from doing so now.

The case dragged on. Finally, in 1980, the Court gave its decision. It began with a blockbuster development.

"Mr. Morales is a thirty-seven-year-old married male alien. Since filing his application to remain and since the institution of this procedure, Mr. Morales has married a lawful permanent resident in November 1979. He has testified that he is living with his wife in a 'normal husband and wife relationship'."

"The evidence presented earlier in this case is that Mr Morales is a homosexual based on a statement taken from him concerning 'certain sexual experiences as well as an opinion from the Public Health Service.' However, he has presented the expert testimony of Dr. Richard Green in opposition to the Public Health Service opinion. Their opinion was that Mr Morales was afflicted with psychopathic personality—sexual deviation for homosexuality."

"The marriage of Mr. Morales suggests there may be some infirmity in the conclusion recorded by the

Public Health Service concerning his basic sexual orientation. Consequently, the government has not sustained the burden of showing by clear and convincing and unequivocal evidence that Mr. Morales was, at the time of his entry, a sexual deviate and excludable as a psychopathic personality." (8)

That conclusion had been reached 17 years earlier.

TEN

ADOPTION BY HOMOSEXUAL PARENTS

"Should Homosexuals Adopt Children? The Burden of Proof Is On Those Who Say No". This was the title of my chapter in the 1978 text *Controversy in Psychiatry*. (1)

Controversy? There wasn't much in 1978 – very few would approve. (2) I don't know why I was asked to contribute to this edited book. Perhaps I was the only contributor who would provide a qualified "yes".

The issue was complex. Was there evidence that homosexuals are better or worse at parenting? Was the prospective parent male or female, single or coupled? What might the effects be on the development of the child? How old was the child? Was it a boy or a girl? To what extent would the child be stigmatized?

When a question is asked about a heterosexual prospective adoptive parent the focus is on the attributes of that adult. But here there was focus on an entire group. Adoptive parenthood requires effective parenting skills and commitment to the well-being of the child. Was there evidence of a character defect in the homosexual so as to compromise these requirements? My research had looked at currently homosexually-active parents who previously functioned as parents in a male-female union. There was no evidence that they were less adequate as parents. (3)

Whether homosexuality is itself a mental disorder had been essentially put to rest with its deletion from the psychiatric manual of disorders. (4) The picture of universal homosexual psychopathology by a hard core of psychoanalysts was a minority view. Recent studies comparing heterosexual with homosexual non-patients found essentially no differences on a wide range of psychological functioning. (5) No picture developed of a person psychologically unfit to parent.

Although the male-female parent family had been traditionally seen as providing the appropriate role model for young children, there had been a dramatic rise in the divorce rate and the number of children in female-only households. This had not increased the rates of homosexuality, if that was a concern.

Whether a child was being raised in a one or two parent household was significant. For a single male, sufficient time to care for a young child can be challenging, but not necessarily more so than for a single female. The age of the child poses different time requirements. An adoptive parent in a child-sharing relationship with another adult would be better prepared for the additional time investment in very young children. But these issues had nothing to do with the adoptive parent's sexuality.

Adoption agencies were concerned about stigma for the child. Peer group teasing because of the homosexual parent household was a worry. However, few children escape some degree of teasing. Some are taunted about religion, race, being overweight, intelligence level, athletic prowess (lack of). Would this type of teasing be any more traumatic?

Geography could be a factor: urban or rural, conservative or liberal? On the positive side was the changing public attitude toward homosexuality. Younger generations, particularly, had become more accepting.

There was another worry: Do homosexual parents want their children to be gay? I wrote, "Not the ones I interviewed. They want their children to be happy. It is easier to be heterosexual. When pressed as to whether they would try to proselytize their child into homosexuality, they typically responded, 'If I wanted to, I wouldn't know how'. Neither does the author of this essay."

I concluded: "Those who would deny homosexuals adoption, based on sexual orientation, bear the burden of proving that such persons make unfit parents."

The bad news: During the year this chapter was written (1978) Florida banned adoption by gays and lesbians. (6) It took thirty-three years for the ban to be overturned as unconstitutional.

The good news: In the next year I submitted an affidavit for two gay men in California to co-adopt a child. It was a landmark success.

Thirteen years later, the American Psychological Association endorsed adoption of children by same-sex couples.

ELEVEN

GAYS IN THE MILITARY?

In 1987, Joseph Steffan was a star midshipman at the United States Naval Academy, the training facility for naval officers. He was twice chosen to sing the national anthem as a soloist at the televised annual Army-Navy football game.

In March, he informed someone that he was homosexual. A few weeks before expected graduation, he was told that he would not graduate. He had "insufficient aptitude to become a commissioned officer in the naval service". His grade in military performance dropped from A to F by reason of homosexuality.

Steffan sued the Department of Defense to obtain his diploma and for a declaration that prohibiting a homosexual from serving in the navy or attending the Naval Academy was unconstitutional. He argued that it was a violation of Equal Protection under the

US Constitution. Thus began a seventeen-year saga of litigation. (1)

The government argued its reasons for barring a homosexual: maintenance of discipline, morale, good order, a respected system of rank and command, a healthy military force, and respect for privacy interests. Prohibition of homosexuality had continued from the Colonial Army in the 18th century to the 20th century Articles of War where it was lumped with forgery, arson and burglary. (2)

I was asked to provide an affidavit in support of Steffan by his volunteer attorney, Marc Wolinsky, who was working with the gay civil rights group Lambda Legal. He adapted a paper I had published in which I argued that homosexuality was an "immutable" characteristic. This was to bolster the argument that sexual orientation, as an inborn or unchangeable feature like race, ethnicity or national origin, was protected by the highest level of constitutional scrutiny. My twenty-five-page statement was submitted in August 1991. The content was also the essence of my in-person testimony in the Colorado Constitutional Amendment trial challenging the Colorado law limiting civil rights for gays and lesbians, described in Section 14. (3)

I argued that homosexual orientation is not consciously chosen, but rather that sexual feelings are a basic part of an individual's psyche and established in early childhood. I described studies showing that sexual orientation is largely influenced by genetic, hormonal, and other factors prior to birth. Furthermore, clinical research showed that, whatever the origins of homosexuality, attempts at "reorientation" of individuals with a homosexual orientation to heterosexuality had poor results. A variety of treatment strategies to convert a homosexual person had failed. These included long-term psychoanalysis, and aversion treatment (electric shocks paired with homosexual imagery). Only a small number of patients reported some reduction in homosexual arousal and some new heterosexual arousal.

In response, the military argued that I acknowledged that "changes in sexual orientation have frequently occurred as a result of therapy". My reply was that these studies, when examined critically, revealed "substantial defects in their methodology, and follow-up data tend to show that these 'conversions' either did not actually take place or were temporary." Further, a psychiatrist who spent years attempting to change sexual orientation with electric shocks in one hundred fifty-seven males concluded that this treatment did not alter basic sexual orientation. (4)

Similarly unavailing was the military's attempt to rely on my own work with cross-gender behaving boys for the conclusion that changes in homosexual orientation "have frequently occurred as a result of therapy". As the military noted, three-quarters of my group of feminine-behaving young boys studied over a period of fifteen years were homosexual or bisexual in adulthood. "This does not mean, however, that the remaining twenty-five per cent were 'converted' from a homosexual orientation to a heterosexual orientation, as the military claims. The fallacy here is the contention that all of the boys were in fact pre-homosexual. There is no basis for this." The military also ignored the fact that one-third of the boys were in psychotherapy. "The rate of later homosexual or bisexual orientation in the 'treated' group was the same as the 'untreated' group." (5)

As an update, I discussed research published after my affidavit demonstrating a brain difference in homosexual males. It was from the neuroscientist Simon LeVay who studied the volume of cells in a region of the anterior hypothalamus in the brain. It was more than twice as large in the heterosexual men. (6)

The argument for immutability did not sway the court. The judge acknowledged, "whether homosexual orientation is an immutable characteristic is difficult to analyse. The court is convinced that homosexual orientation is neither conclusively mutable nor immutable since the scientific community is still quite at sea." However, the court sailed toward one coast. "It is not for this Court to say definitively whether sexual orientation is always chosen by the individual. But it is apparent that sometimes it is chosen." (7)

Steffan was arguing before an unfriendly judge. Twice he was referred to as a "homo". (8) When his attorney asked for access to part of a document reporting on homosexuals serving in the military, the judge objected to including sections that might relate to every "homo" that may be walking the face of the earth. In another exchange, he referred to Steffan's affidavit stating that he is a homosexual and knows other homosexuals serving in the military, as the section where he says he is a "homo" and knows other "homos". These comments appeared in the *New York Times,* the *Wall Street Journal,* the *Washington Post* and the *Los Angeles Times.* The government argued that "homo" is not a derogatory term. An effort to replace the judge was unsuccessful. Steffan lost before this judge and his case was dismissed. He appealed and secured a reversal. (9)

In a new trial, a "friend of the court" statement by a non-party to the litigation was submitted by the American Naval Aviation Foundation. It provided an imposing list of attributes required by a midshipman: "virtue, honor, courage, patriotism, self-sacrifice, discipline, honesty, authority, subordination, faithfulness, temperance, chastity, fidelity, and duty. The midshipman's military life, as well as his social and family life, is always expected to fully reflect those character traits."(10) No more, no less.

Steffan lost again. The ruling was that the exclusion of homosexuals from the military rationally furthered a legitimate government purpose because it protected service members from AIDS. A three-judge panel of the Court of Appeals reversed the decision. It ordered the Navy to commission Steffan as an officer and grant a Naval Academy diploma. Remarkably, the court held that the Equal Protection guarantee of the Constitution did not permit the government to terminate an armed service member merely by their saying they were homosexual. However, at the time, the "Don't ask, don't tell" policy of President Clinton was in effect. That did provide for dismissal if the service person told.

The Chief Justice on the three-judge panel, Abner Mikva, wrote, "The Constitution does not allow Government to subordinate a class of person simply because others do not like them. America's hallmark has been to judge people by what they do and not by who they are." (11) Reflecting on his career, he said that this was his proudest court statement. The next year Mikva became White House Counsel to President Clinton.

The government did not throw in the towel. Since the Court of Appeals had ordered that Steffan be awarded his naval commission, they argued that only the President, with the consent of the Senate, could award a commission. The order was suspended.

The case was then heard by the full Court of Appeals in May 1994. In November, the court, by a 7-3 majority, awarded victory to the government. (12) All seven justices in the majority had been appointed by Republican Presidents Reagan or Bush. The three dissenters were appointed by Democrat Presidents Carter or Clinton. Steffan did not appeal to the Supreme Court. He went to law school and became a practicing attorney in New York City.

In 1987, when the Steffan case began, many countries accepted homosexual men and women in military service. These included Australia, Belgium, France, Germany, Israel, Portugal, Spain, Sweden, and the Netherlands.

In 2011, the United States dropped its ban on openly homosexual service personnel. (13)

SINGING NATIONAL ANTHEM

TWELVE

MORALLY STRAIGHT: THE BOY SCOUT CREDO

"On my honor I will do my best…to keep myself… morally straight." (1)

When I took the Boy Scout oath as a teen in Brooklyn I parroted these words, not knowing precisely what they meant. Decades later they were at the core of the first court case in which I was an attorney. I did not know that "morally straight" meant heterosexual. It would not have occurred to me that it barred a homosexual. But, back then, I did not know any homosexuals (or so I thought).

The Boy Scout case welcomed me as a lawyer. Attending law school had been a twenty-seven-year deferral. As a pre-medical student, I flirted with law. I took the Law School Admissions Test. But the pinnacle kvell (boast) of a Brooklyn Jewish household was "My son, the doctor". There had been none in my extended family. Wall to wall lawyers, yes, but doctors, no. Law schools welcomed Jewish applicants. Not medical schools. Johns Hopkins admitted me as one of the ten per cent maximum. The challenge to attend medical school was greater.

Years as a psychiatric court witness in sex and gender cases, working with dozens of lawyers, convinced me that I could do as well as a lawyer, maybe better. I would extend my work as a psychiatric witness to representing sex and gender minorities as an attorney. And my family planning was more practical than my dad's. He had gone to law school, but graduated during the depression and had a wife and kid (me). He never practiced. At the time, I had no wife and no kid. So, at fifty, I applied to Harvard and Yale. Fortunately, Harvard said "no". Yale is smaller, more informal, less stressful, and more philosophical and theoretical in training one to "think like a lawyer".

Compared to med school, law was a stroll. I finished all the written required projects in the first two of three years, and won the Moot Court elimination competition against all students with my final argument before a panel of federal judges. I never worried about failing because I already had a career. Had I been dropped from med school my most frequent statement could have been, "Would you like fries with that?"

From Yale, I returned to California to intern with a federal appeals court judge and knock down the remaining class hours of the third year. But, I was not done yet. For licensing, California was a target of law school graduates looking toward palm trees. To prevent a tsunami of attorneys, they concocted a treacherous multi-day exam. To make it worse yet, Yale prided itself on not preparing graduates for the real world of law practice. California examined on thirteen subjects. Six had not been taught at Yale. After two months of industrial strength "review" classes, it was now also "My son the lawyer". My "audience of one" never knew. My dad died about a decade earlier.

I became a volunteer attorney with the American Civil Liberties Union. Since 1980, before I had enrolled at Yale, the ACLU had been engaged in a case representing Tim Curran. (2) Curran had been an exemplary scout as a teen and aspired to be an assistant scoutmaster. But he had taken a male date to his high school senior prom. The Boy Scouts sprang into action. He was barred.

California had a civil rights act named for the popular liberal attorney general Jesse Unruh. He had been Robert Kennedy's California campaign manager during his run for president that ended in assassination. The Unruh Civil Rights Act of 1959 barred any business establishment from discriminating on age, color, national origin, race, or religion. (3) Sexual orientation was not added specifically until 2005, but earlier cases indicated this to be included. (4)

We at the ACLU were convinced that the Scouts were a business establishment. They had a budget of nearly two million dollars a year, twenty-two full-time employees, and operated a retail shop selling uniforms and equipment.

With experienced attorneys Jon Davidson and Paul Hoffman, I prepared for my first court hearing. Along with their legal argument that the Scouts were a business, and therefore in non-compliance with the law, I would present evidence about homosexuality. This was my opportunity to call my first witness in a court of law. It was Judd Marmor. As described earlier, he had been the most prominent psychiatrist arguing for delisting homosexuality as a mental disorder. (5) As a President of the American Psychiatric Association, he had more visibility in that campaign than I. With considerable stage fright, I examined (interviewed) Judd on the witness stand in September 1990.

Virgin attorney: "Dr. Marmor, based on your fifty years of clinical experience in psychiatry, do you have an opinion on when sexual orientation is fixed?"

Dr. Marmor: "I think it is pretty well fixed before the age of six or seven."

Attorney: "And on what do you base that opinion?"

Marmor: "Research shows there may well be a genetic predisposition to homosexuality. That would be prenatal. Homosexual patients I have worked with have reported that very early on in their childhood, in their third, fourth, fifth years, they were aware of a significant difference in the way they felt towards men—toward little boys and girls, compared to others of their peers."

Attorney: "Are there studies of children who become homosexual that also add to your view?"

Marmor: "Yes. Prospective studies observe children who are cross-gendered in behavior and then follow them later in life. These predisposed children in two-thirds to three-quarters become openly homosexual." (This was what my research found.)

Attorney: "Based on your clinical experience, do you have an opinion whether having an openly homosexual scoutmaster would increase the probability of scouts later developing a homosexual orientation?"

Marmor: "There is no evidence that sexual orientation is determined at that point in life. It has already been predetermined."

Attorney: "Assume, if you will, just hypothetically, that having an openly homosexual scoutmaster would increase homosexual experimentation by the scouts. Do you have an opinion whether this would increase the likelihood that the scouts would become homosexual as adults?"

Marmor: "No, it would not. Because the fifty per cent of the heterosexual boys who do involve themselves in same sex activity--the vast majority of them go on to function as heterosexuals, and only a small percentage whom we have reason to think have a predisposition are the ones who go on to become homosexual."

Attorney: "Do you have an opinion whether having an openly homosexual scoutmaster would increase the scout's anxiety about sexuality?"

Marmor: "It would not. Let's look at it in terms of the two groups of children. Those who are possibly predisposed to being homosexual, and those who are presumably going ahead in a heterosexual direction. Those who are predisposed are often tortured by the feeling that they are different—they don't fully understand it. They feel debased by the discrimination and the jokes that are passed about homosexuals. And for them, seeing an adult scoutmaster who is functioning in a responsible and mature and admirable way would do a great deal to enhance their self-image and reduce their anxiety. For the heterosexuals, it would reduce the prejudice and superstition and stereotyping of homosexuals that is so widespread".

Attorney: "How do you understand the concept of role modelling?"

Marmor: "It has to do with certain kinds of values, things that are incorporated from models whom the child grows up with and admires. I know of no evidence that role modelling causes sexual orientation, because that is already well set long before that kind of role modelling takes place. Moreover, the role models are at least ninety-five per cent heterosexual."

Attorney: "Are parents role models?"

Marmor: "Yes."

Attorney: "Are you familiar with studies of the children of homosexual parents?"

Marmor: "Yes, one major study. Of forty homosexual fathers with twenty-three sons, only one was homosexual. Three quarters knew from their early years that their father was homosexual."

Attorney: "Is homosexuality considered by modern psychiatry to be a mental illness?"

Marmor: "No, it is not. Not since 1973 when the American Psychiatric Association took it out of the manual of disorders."

Attorney: "Thank you, Professor Marmor." (Long exhale.)

My co-counsel advanced legal logic about what constituted a business establishment, and why the Scouts qualified. The Boy Scouts argued that since its incorporation in the early 1900s they considered homosexuality to be immoral.

The trial court had a mixed ruling. The Scouts did fall under the anti-discrimination provisions of the Unruh Act. However, the Scouts had a Constitutional First Amendment right to express their view of homosexuality by their membership. This trumped the business establishment finding. (6)

The case was appealed. We were nailed on both counts. The appellate court, by a 2-1 majority, held that the Scouts were not a business establishment. And, nailing shut the coffin, it held that even if it were a business, the federal Constitutional guarantee of freedom of expression, speech, and association prevailed over any state law. (7)

This ruling appeared to turn anti-discrimination law on its head. As the Scouts had a long tradition of advocating what they hold to be appropriate sexuality, their right to discriminate prevailed.

The California Supreme Court heard the case on further appeal after I moved to London. Jon continued as counsel. Mysteriously, when reviewing previous decisions, the Court bestowed me with the middle initial "H".

The Court held that it was not necessary to rule on the First Amendment issue of free expression because the Scouts were not a business. (8) As the Court saw it, the Scouts had no substantial business purpose and the goals of scouting were predominantly fostering and teaching their moral principals. The benefits to scouts were personal and not economic. The sales of goods in its shops were to its members and not the general public.

This decision was less than straightforward. A Supreme Court justice observed, "To put it bluntly, the law is a mess. Our prior decisions have almost universally failed to formulate a coherent and comprehensive interpretation of 'business establishment'." (9)

After our unsuccessful challenge, there was backlash against the Scouts. Prominent California financial contributors withdrew. They included Levi Strauss (the jean maker), Wells Fargo (the bank), and the San Francisco chapter of United Way, the coalition of charitable organizations that raises five billion dollars a year.

There were other Boy Scout cases. The New Jersey Supreme Court ruled that the Scouts could not bar a homosexual scout leader. The decision was appealed to the US Supreme Court in 2000. By 5-4 it ruled in favor of the Scouts. (10) Liberal justices Stevens, Souter, Ginsburg, and Breyer needed one more vote, but could not persuade potential swing voters Kennedy or O'Connor. There was no hope with conservatives Rehnquist, Scalia, or Thomas.

Then, in 2013, the Scouts, bowing to growing public opposition, dropped its ban on gay youth members, but continued to bar gay leaders. Two years later it rescinded its ban on leaders. However, it allowed religious organizations that operate two-thirds of scouting units to use religious-based criteria, including sexuality, for selecting adult leaders. (11)

At least the leaders were morally straight.

THE AUTHOR: MORALLY STRAIGHT

THIRTEEN

CRUSADE IN ORANGE

Anita Bryant was the face on the Florida orange. Nationally televised commercials featured her singing "Come to the Florida Sunshine Tree".

She was a runner up in the 1959 Miss America contest. She had been a singer of modest success (one record rose to number five in 1960). She sang the national anthem at a Super Bowl football match. She sang for President Johnson at the White House. And she was also a fundamentalist Christian who wrote nine religious books that sold a total of one million copies. She condemned homosexual "sinfulness". (1)

Dade County, Florida, which had a substantial gay and lesbian population in the Miami Coconut Grove area, passed an ordinance in 1977 ensuring equal rights for homosexual men and women. It barred discrimination in jobs, housing, and public accommodation. By then, the American Psychiatric Association had delisted homosexuality as a mental disorder. (2) Momentum was gathering at the national level for increased understanding and acceptance, if not a full embrace, of homosexual men and women.

But, to Anita Bryant, this had to be halted. She organized a crusade against gay rights. "What these people really want, hidden behind obscure legal phrases, is the legal right to propose to our children that there is an acceptable alternate way of life. I will lead such a crusade to stop it as this country has not seen before." (3)

The crusade was "Save Our Children", invoking the bogeyman of the homosexual child recruiter and molester. This "because of my love for the Almighty God, because of my love for His Word, because of my love for my Country, because of the love for my children. As a mother, I know that homosexuals cannot biologically reproduce children, therefore, they must recruit our children." (Anita's "vampire theory".) (3)

She was creative in her arguments: "Homosexuals are called 'fruits' because they eat the forbidden fruit of the tree of life...which is male sperm." (The tree of life was not forbidden in Eden, only the tree of the knowledge of good and evil. There are no female sperm.) She used humor, "If homosexuality were normal, God would have created Adam and Bruce" and "If gays are granted rights, next we'll have to give rights to prostitutes, to people who sleep with St. Bernards, and to nailbiters." (3)

Bryant organized a referendum for a popular vote to repeal the equal rights protection. The anti-gay referendum had strong support from Southern

Baptists, but less from the retired Jewish residents of Miami and Miami Beach. Support came from the conservative Cuban community but less from black residents. The Catholic Church was less engaged as they were worrying about some of their priests abusing children. (1)

It was the first nationally reported US controversy over gay civil rights. Television networks sent crews for nightly reporting. The *New York Times*, the *Washington Post* and the *Los Angeles Times* sent reporters.

The *Washington Post* called the Bryant campaign a "full-fledged extremist movement with a particular appeal to bigotry". A pivotal argument in the crusade was the harm to children from exposure to gay teachers. The *New York Times* dismissed this fear, but few copies of that paper were sold in Dade County.

The founder of the National Gay Task Force was Bruce Voeller, who I testified for in his unsuccessful attempt to have joint child custody after divorce (Section 7). He wrote, "In a single year Bryant exposed more Americans to the gay issue than our movement had done in a decade. Bryant gave us our first massive national opportunity to put our case before the public." (4)

The atmosphere was hotter in Miami than usual. T-shirts were sold with the slogan, "Squeeze a Fruit for Anita", and badges read "Anita Bryant Sucks Oranges".

Because of Bryant's insistence that homosexuals were recruiting young people to their sinful way of life, opponents of the referendum invited me, John Money, and a past-president of the American Psychiatric Association, John Spiegel, to Miami to hold a press conference.

The press release by the Dade County Coalition for Human Rights announced our statement:

"We, as people whose careers are dedicated to helping others achieve productive, happy and healthy lives through medicine, psychiatry, and science, affirm that as a group within our society, homosexuals are responsible, mature, productive, and well-adjusted. Homosexuality has nothing to do with child molesting. The overwhelming number of instances of child molestation are committed by adult males with girls. A high proportion involve fathers, brothers, and uncles, not strangers lurking."

"Regarding the alleged 'danger' of homosexuals as role models, a claim has been made that children will tend to become homosexual if they have a teacher who is an 'open' homosexual. No child can be influenced or recruited in such a way as to alter that child's sexual orientation. Virtually all people who express a homosexual inclination as adults went through school systems where any homosexual teachers would not dare acknowledge their homosexuality for fear of losing their jobs. Therefore, people who today are adult homosexuals had presumably heterosexual teachers as 'role models', not to speak of the child's parents."

"In sum, homosexuals are not child molesters, homosexuals as 'role models' do not influence children's sexual orientation, and homosexuals are capable of being productive and responsible members of society. The basic issue is a simple matter of prejudice and discrimination versus human rights, and we are hopeful that the people of Dade County will decide in favor of human rights for all people." (5)

We were very well received by the audience of reporters who smiled and nodded their heads. The general public was less impressed. The referendum passed by a 2:1 majority.

In retaliation, gay bars removed the screwdriver drink made with orange juice and vodka from their list of cocktails, and concocted one with apple juice and vodka. It was the "Anita Bryant".

Her career and marriage went into free-fall. In an October 1977 televised press conference, Bryant was hit in the face with a large banana cream pie by a gay rights activist. She quipped, "Well, at least it's a fruit pie". Having declared in 1978 that "divorce" was not a word in her vocabulary (6), two years later she ended her marriage.

Negative publicity for Bryant was increasing at the national level. The Florida Citrus Association squeezed her out of her $100,000 a year role as their national brand ambassador.

Nevertheless, the successful Bryant crusade encouraged other legislation. Six months after our defeat, a California constitutional amendment was put to vote that would bar gay people or anyone advancing a homosexual lifestyle from teaching. It failed. However, Oklahoma did enact a "Teacher fitness" law whereby local schools could fire homosexual teachers or any teacher advocating, encouraging, or promoting homosexual activities.

It was twenty years before Dade County reauthorized an anti-discrimination ordinance protecting homosexual men and women. (7)

FOURTEEN

APRES SKI: COLORADO

In 1992, Colorado was a great place in the US to ski (still is). The general state population wasn't particularly anti-homosexual. But some local pro-gay communities were enacting antidiscrimination ordinances. Others saw this as special legal treatment for gays (affirmative action) and argued that it discriminated against heterosexuals. At the time, nationally, homosexuality was disapproved of. Two-thirds of Americans agreed with the statement "Homosexual relations are always wrong." (1)

An amendment to the state constitution, Amendment 2, was put to ballot by the right-wing religious group Colorado for Family Values. The amendment read "…homosexual, lesbian or bisexual orientation, conduct, practices or relationships (shall not) entitle any person or class of persons to have or claim any minority status, quota preferences, protected status or claim of discrimination." (2) Fifty-three per cent of voters approved.

A lengthy legal battle followed. A book reporting the trial that capped this episode states: "Although this was not the first trial to address an anti-gay attack, it was the most comprehensive in its attempt to sift through all that was known about gay people from ancient history through the latest scientific research." (3)

A Constitutional challenge to the Amendment could be that it is an infringement on a "fundamental right" where there must be a compelling state interest, narrowly tailored. Or, it could be an "equal protection" argument where a governmental discrimination is inherently suspect when it targets a specific class of people (they are a "suspect class"). The legal standard is the same as for a "fundamental right".

Amendment 2 was challenged in state trial court in November 1992, and a temporary injunction prevented enforcement. Attorneys fighting the Amendment decided to go to trial without a jury arguing, among other issues, that homosexual people were a "suspect class". To qualify, the trait for which they are disadvantaged is inborn and unchangeable (immutable). Race, ethnicity and national origin are examples. The trial outcome was expected to be appealed to the Colorado Supreme Court and then on to the US Supreme Court. (4) I was invited to testify. I was to educate the court about homosexuality and address whether it was immutable.

An attorney working with us challenging the Amendment, Ruth Harlow, had been with me at Yale law school. She authored the "friend of the court" document in the case for the American Bar Association. Later she was lead counsel in the landmark case before the US Supreme Court that invalidated laws criminalizing homosexuality. Another expert witness was to be my Yale constitutional law professor, an expert on civil rights, Burke Marshall. He had helped draft the Civil Rights Act of 1964 protecting racial minorities. A last minute effort to defeat its passage was tacking on an anti-sex discrimination act. The strategy failed. They were both enacted. And there was to be the usual cast of "unusual suspects", Judd Marmor, with me, vs. Charles Socarides.

I was an "odd choice" selection by the legal team fighting to overturn Amendment 2, according to the book documenting the trial. Allegedly, I claimed that many gay men could be identified as gay in boyhood through a simple blood test for hormone levels. (5) This is a complete fiction. Had I been aware of this decades earlier (I had not read the book on publication, but only recently) I would have demanded a retraction. According to the book, a psychologist colleague, James Weinrich, was quoted in the *Washington Blade*, a gay newspaper, referring to my work, "If you don't want a queer son, get this injection." James told me years later that he had no idea based on my research why he would have said it, that I never advocated any such thing, and thinks the quote referred to something else. (6)

There was also concern about my research demonstrating that the great majority of prepubertal boys showing extensive cross-gender behavior matured as homosexual men. This, the objectors argued, contributed to a disfavored stereotype. The finding has been reported by others. (7)

My testimony was announced in the *Denver Post*. "Dr. Richard Green, professor of psychiatry at the University of California School of Medicine, will testify that homosexual orientation is not consciously chosen, but rather that sexual feelings are a basic part of an individual's psyche and are established in childhood." (8)

Much of what I testified to was the inborn, unchangeable nature of homosexual orientation. I explained the growing body of supporting biological research. There were twin studies with fifty per cent concordance for homosexuality between genetically identical twins. That it was not one hundred per cent was not all that surprising, however. Not all prenatal events are identical. Birth weights of twins differ. Parents can identify the individual co-twins. Fifty per cent was much higher than among non-identical twins or non-twin siblings. Additionally, studies of females with a condition producing excessive male hormone before birth found higher rates of homosexual and bisexual fantasy and behavior. And four brain anatomy studies found differences between heterosexual and homosexual males.

My research with cross-gender behaving boys not only showed behavioral features that could predict adult homosexuality (an argument against an adult "choice" of sexual orientation) but also that treatments of some of these boys by other clinicians to modify later sexual orientation were ineffective.

I acknowledged that there were a "handful" of people who claimed they can change a homosexual orientation to heterosexual. However, "these people are refuted by most professionals." I argued that even if homosexuality could be modified in some, it did not mean that it was not inborn. Left-handedness, reflecting an inborn dominant right brain hemisphere, could be altered (perhaps with the consequence of a stammer).

TESTIFYING

As reported in the *Denver Post*, I emphasized the difference between sexual orientation and sexual behavior. (9) Choosing a pattern of behavior is not necessarily one's orientation and is more modifiable.

A person with a heterosexual orientation may engage in homosexual conduct under some circumstances, such as prison.

Colorado for Family Values fired off the predictable defense of limiting the rights of homosexual citizens—they pose a threat to children. I testified that my research and that of others found that homosexual parents are "no better, no worse" than heterosexual parents and that my study of lesbian mothers showed that their children did not differ in psychological health from children of heterosexual mothers.

We knew that the State, arguing gay people pose a threat to children, would call as a witness, Paul Cameron. For decades he had led a crusade reporting that homosexuals were mentally ill and posed a threat to children. His research was usually published in his organization's journal. Cameron's research and conclusions were so outrageous that the American Psychological Association dropped him from membership in 1983 for violation of ethical principles. (10) Three years later the American Sociological Association "repudiated any claim that Paul Cameron is a sociologist and condemned his misrepresentation of sociological research." (11) I testified that Cameron's "findings" were at odds with other researchers. The State decided not to call him as a witness.

I was asked about Charles Socarides, who had submitted an affidavit and was expected to testify. To that psychoanalyst, a homosexual has a "psychiatric psychopathology". A gay son has no "appropriate masculine role model".

WOW!! Socarides' son was gay. He served as advisor on gay issues to President Clinton.

I testified that Charles' views did not represent those of the mainstream of his professions, psychiatry and psychoanalysis. The state did not call him as a witness. He was advised not to testify by his son. (12)

Judd Marmor was challenged as a witness for having written earlier that homosexuality had environmental influences and was modifiable. He countered adroitly, "I think a good scientist should be able to change his mind with new evidence. The more I know, the more I'm going to change my mind."

The case was argued before the US Supreme Court in October 1995. The court ruled in May 1996 by a 6-3 vote that Amendment 2 was unconstitutional. The majority opinion was written by swing vote Anthony Kennedy (a Justice who can vote liberal or conservative) and joined by another swing vote, O'Connor, and the liberal wing of Stevens, Souter, Ginsburg and Breyer.

The analysis differed from the state courts. "Strict scrutiny" of a "suspect class" (the most exacting level of protection) was not applied. The Amendment targeting homosexuals was based on animosity and lacked a rational basis to a legitimate governmental purpose. The Amendment imposed a special disability upon homosexuals. "If the constitutional conception of equal protection of the laws means anything, it must at the very least mean that a bare...desire to harm a politically unpopular group cannot constitute a legitimate governmental interest."

The conservative Court wing of Scalia, Rehnquist, and Thomas was furious. "The Court has mistaken Kulturkampf for a fit of spite. It is no business for the courts (as opposed to the political branches) to take sides in the culture war. But the Court today has done so... by verbally disparaging as bigotry adherence to traditional attitudes." (13)

Seven hours of evidence on "immutability" was invisible in the Supreme Court decision.

Around this time, the city of Cincinnati, Ohio, enacted similar legislation. It, too, bounced between courts. Eventually, a petition to the Supreme Court to overrule the latest ruling permitting the legislation was denied. The interpretation of this refusal to hear the case was characterized by some as a "distinction without a difference". The Cincinnati law was local, whereas the Colorado amendment was state-wide. Many were puzzled why an unconstitutional law at the state level could be permissible locally.

Later, Colorado passed a law forbidding discrimination in employment based on sexual orientation and gender identity. Fifteen years later. (14)

Part 2

TRANSSEXUALISM

FIFTEEN

EX-GI BECOMES BLOND BEAUTY

This was the tabloid *New York Daily News* banner headline of December 1, 1952. Pictured below were George Jorgensen (then) and Christine Jorgensen (now). "Sex change" took place in Denmark, the home of Jorgensen's grandparents. (1)

The story changed many lives, including mine. For thousands of others it gave hope to those convinced they were trapped in the body of the wrong sex. For me it ignited a career. I was sixteen, nearing decision time for college, and what I wanted to do in life. I would discuss this with my dad. When the Christine news hit and immediately became a sensation, I asked him, "Why can't everyone else's curiosity be one person's career?" My dad-- "There's no reason why it can't be." I had permission.

Christine was "Woman of the Year" in 1953. Wire services quickly followed the *Daily News* headline with 50,000 words. She was paid $25,000 for her story by the Hearst Sunday newspaper supplement, *American Weekly.* That would be a quarter of a million dollars today.

Dr. Harry Benjamin was emerging as the "Father of Transsexualism". He understood the misery of those who needed to change sex, and, in the 1950s, had begun treating American transsexuals when no other physicians were. One was Christine, after her return to the US.

Harry was concerned by the swarm of publicity over her transformation and expressed this to Christine in a letter. "I am worried over the effect of your story and publicity. I have frantic phone calls and letters. I would be grateful if you care telling me how you are handling the innumerable communications that undoubtedly come to you. Don't they all indicate hopefulness yet utter frustration? Can I tell them that you will answer their pleas with a personal, friendly non-committal form letter, perhaps for psychological reasons, bearing your signature?"

In the mid-1960s, when I was seeing transsexual patients with Harry, he offered to introduce me to Christine. He arranged my visit when she was living with her mother who had advanced breast cancer. Christine was very welcoming and encouraged me in my research. She told me that she would be politically active for the transsexual cause.

While visiting the home of her Danish physician, Christian Hamburger, who steered her treatment, I was shown a large hall closet. It had been overflowing with letters from desperate people from many countries pleading for his help. To preserve the national medical budget, Denmark passed a law permitting the procedures for Danish citizens only. Christine named herself (as a woman) after her physician, Christian.

The Christine Jorgensen Story was the 1970 film version of her autobiography. In that book, she described a childhood that became the prototype for males who followed her, desperately seeking "sex change". Boys' clothes were hated. An older sister's clothes were admired. Rough-and-tumble games were avoided. "I was a female trapped in a male body." When reaching teenage, romantic and sexual interests were directed toward males. Before filming, Harry, Christine and I met with the producer. We provided considerable advice. All unheeded. Years later, Christine sued the film company, United Artists, for trying to market the film as a "campy B movie." She contended, "It is a classic."

Christine starred in the off-Broadway production of *Oh Dad, Poor Dad, Mamma's Hung You in the Closet and I'm Feelin' So Sad.* I thought she was good. She toured nationally and appeared in many nightclubs. Her signature song: "I Enjoy Being a Girl".

Christine was regularly featured on college campuses and spoke to a hundred thousand students. I watched her give an hour-long lecture to a packed audience of UCLA students in 1972 in which she credited my research program. She was pleased that I had arranged for the first transsexual surgery at UCLA, and approved of our research (trying to understand how the urgent need for transsexual treatment evolved from childhood and whether it could be prevented).

Sometimes cancer runs in families. Christine asked that, at her death, friends and relations remember her with a lavish party. In historian Joanne Myerowitz's text, *How Sex Changed,* she writes "around 150 guests attended, including Richard Green." (2)

It must have been lavish. I have no memory of the event.

CHRISTINE COMES HOME

WITH CHRISTINE: SHE'S
ON THE RIGHT

SIXTEEN

BRAVE NEW MEDICAL WORLD

In the 1960s, a brave new medical world was evolving in the New York office of Dr. Harry Benjamin. Harry was in his fifties (halfway through his life span) when Alfred Kinsey, sex history interviewer of thousands, referred a man who wanted to become a woman. Harry listened sympathetically to the man's plight. Although a few patients with this aspiration had been treated in Europe in the 1930s, in the US they were medical orphans because no one would help them.

Word in this underground community quickly spread. There was a doctor who understood their needs and was prepared to help. By 1965, Harry had 250 patients who were dissatisfied with the sex into which they were born.

Harry's previous practice was treating older age patients. He believed that procaine injections (an anesthetic) fended off the deterioration of ageing.

He injected himself. And he did live past 100. But his parents approached the century mark without procaine.

After John Money introduced us in 1965, Harry invited me to sit in on his Saturday New York office hours. He was of average height, mostly bald, a bit overweight, wore a long white lab coat, and spoke with a German accent, having been born in Berlin. Harry was a fatherly listener and would administer cross-sex hormones, usually female hormone injections as most of the patients were born male. With his tape measure he would meticulously chart the gradual growth of breast tissue.

A prerogative of being a medical doctor was permission to examine the genitalia of a female who was not one's partner. Harry "seduced" me into his world when I examined Janet who had recently returned from Casablanca where the surgeon George Burou transformed male into female genitals. Burou was the foremost sex-change surgeon. Once payment made its way into his confidential Swiss bank account, he worked his surgical magic.

Janet's genitalia looked indistinguishable from a born female. Additionally, she was very attractive and bore no hint of having been male. Harry took both of us for dinner to a posh Manhattan restaurant. We were stared at as we walked to our table, not because our woman companion looked freakish, but because she was stunning.

Actually, I was won over before I was "seduced". As difficult as it was to be a homosexual back then, it was much worse to be a transsexual. While desire for love and sex could be part of daily life, being convinced that your body was the wrong sex and you were living as the wrong person was a fulltime nightmare. These people were desperate to bring their body into symmetry with their mind's self image. But where were the helpful physicians and medical facilities?

Another patient of Harry was a teaching lesson in the failure of psychiatric treatment to "cure" transsexualism. This patient's family was therapy-savvy, and when their adolescent son announced that he wanted to live as a woman, he was despatched to a psychoanalyst. Four years later, and continuing with his desire to change sex, he was despatched to another analyst. At the end of his eight years on the analytic couch, I was interviewing this young eye surgeon, Richard Raskind, in Harry's office. He was there to receive female hormones. In my lectures, I have used Raskind's marathon therapy experience to refute the psychiatric mantra—"If only these patients would engage in serious therapy (psychoanalysis), they would be cured."

Richard Raskind completed treatment and became Renee Richards. (Renee is "reborn" in French.) She was also a tennis star, and the title of her autobiography was genius: *Second Serve*. (1) After surgery she fought to compete as a woman in the US Open (then held at Forest Hills). The tennis association initially refused. She went to court. John Money was her witness testifying that she was a woman.

Renee won in court. As a late, unranked entry in the tournament, she was paired in the first match against Virginia Wade who was Wimbledon champion. She lost on that court.

Harry was writing his pioneering book, *The Transsexual Phenomenon.* It would be the first professional text. He asked me if I would write a chapter on historical and cross-cultural aspects. I knew nothing about either. But after three weeks anchored in a library (no internet yet) I became the world expert. My contribution would be Appendix C in Harry's 1966 classic. (2)

After reading my draft, Harry wrote to me on April 19, 1965, "If we can learn anything from these pages of history and anthropology as to the nature and etiology of transsexualism, it is that it is a constitutional factor appearing more likely than 'conditioning'. It is difficult for me to imagine in all these different tribes and primitive peoples that we would find a weak father image or a smothering mother."

In not the safest manner to assure my career as a fledgling psychiatrist, considering the attitude to "sex change" in America, I wrote letters for Harry's patients to have surgery in Europe. Harry had a trusted colleague in Naples, Italy and in 1965 I referred patients to Professor Francesco Sorrentino.

One referral letter of March 1965 read:

"This twenty-five-year old male has been living as a female for over one year, has been receiving female hormones for over two years, has secured a driver's license and social security card as a female, and is currently employed in two jobs as a female."

"The patient seems to understand the nature of sex reassignment surgery and understands that she cannot bear children post operatively and that intercourse as a "female" may not be either enjoyable nor even possible."

"Unless one defines any person who desires a sex reassignment operation as "psychotic", this patient showed no other evidence of psychosis."

"She does not want any psychotherapy directed toward enhancing her gender role orientation toward male. She has had limited contact with psychiatrists. She has been depressed in the past and is somewhat so now. There have been no attempts at suicide but considers this a likely possibility should she be unable to attain surgery."

Enter Reed (born Rita) Erickson. Reed's philanthropy catalysed transsexual progress in the US. As Rita, she was the first woman graduate in mechanical engineering from Louisiana State University. Her father was a wealthy industrialist and at his death a substantial inheritance fell to Rita. She invested wisely and became a multi-millionaire. Intent on living as a man, Rita transitioned to Reed and received treatment from Harry. He was clearly masculine, a deep voice, and red goatee, but short, having been born female. His partner, Aileen, towered over him.

Reed set up the Erickson Educational Foundation. Among its projects was transsexualism and he funded the Harry Benjamin Foundation. This enabled a group of us to assess a series of Harry's patients and meet in Harry's office on Saturday evenings. We were a handful of academics and clinicians drawn together by an interest in Harry's "transsexual phenomenon". We shared our feelings of injustice for these medical orphans.

In addition to myself:

Henry Guze, a professor and psychologist from the American Academy of Psychotherapies, which he co-founded. He was also a co-founder of the Society for the Scientific Study of Sex, for which he served as president from 1964-1966. That was a decade before my election.

Ruth Rae Doorbar, a psychological test expert. She fell in love with a Jamaican man and left the US to live on that island for her remaining decades. She became a pioneer in Jamaican psychotherapy.

Robert Veit Sherwin, an attorney and expert on sex and the law. He authored the innovative, *Sex and the Statutory Law* in 1949. Another founder of the Society for the Scientific Study of Sex.

Herbert Kupperman, New York University expert on hormone disorders in females. He was a pioneer in identifying the chromosomal sex of intersex infants from examination of any tissue cell.

Leo Wollman, a gynecologist and hypnotherapist. He claimed to have treated 2500 transsexuals.

Wardell Pomeroy, principal co-interviewer with Alfred Kinsey for sex histories of thousands of males and females in the Kinsey reports. Wardell took sex history recording very seriously. He showed me a colossal graph documenting his orgasms, year by year, by category—masturbation, female partner, male partner. Wardell's attempt to promote in himself more homosexual interest was a lesson in the resistance of sexual orientation to change. He had tried to enhance it with several male-male experiences, but it never approached his passion for females.

And, most importantly, because of his position at The Johns Hopkins Hospital, there was John Money.

Additional experts joined the Advisory Group of the Foundation. There was Christian Hamburger, who had orchestrated the transition of Christine Jorgensen, and the prominent physician from the Mayo Clinic and syndicated medical columnist, Walter Alvarez.

Over several months, dozens of transsexual patients were assessed by Foundation members. At a Saturday evening meeting, I presented my year's experience with Foundation patients and other patients seen in Harry's office. There were eight Foundation patients, all born as males, two of whom were post-operative. In Harry's office, I saw thirteen birth males and three birth females. Twelve were post-surgery. Not one post-operative patient expressed regret over having made the decision. All stated they were happier and doing better in their daily lives.

Henry Guze interviewed fifty-one patients. He saw profound problems in self-perception and reported an obscure, barely comprehensible, analysis of personality types. By the time this was published in *Transsexualism and Sex Reassignment* (Green and Money, 1968), Section 18, his report was comprehensible (he had a good editor). (3) He noted that the statement by patients of feeling like a person of the other sex is difficult to verify. "It is at best a simile." I have never understood what it means when stated by a patient, as I am not sure I know what it feels like to be a man.

Ruth Rae Doorbar presented a befuddling set of 139 personality traits assembled from psychology tests with thirty-four patients. Again, perhaps due to good editing, her contribution in *Transsexualism and Sex Reassignment* was comprehensible. (4) She also found a higher occurrence of reportedly homosexual brothers, bisexual fathers, and sisters who were lesbian. This predated much of the family genetic research on homosexuality.

Wardell interviewed sixteen patients and found them to be rigid, moralistic, and isolated. Eleven were Catholic and raised with strict religiosity. Decades later, with Stony Brook University colleagues, I reported a strong Catholic upbringing as possibly requiring a male who might be able to live as homosexual or transsexual to choose the latter to avoid the former. As a woman, she would avoid the Catholic stigma of homosexuality with a male partner. (5)

Wardell also reported the number of sexual partners of his patients. Females wanting to become men had a sex life more like that of males with up to 75 partners. Oddly, males clamoring for removal of their penis reported between 50 and 1,000 partners. Use of their penis, however, was not that frequent, by their report.

The Foundation's work was attracting professional interest. We were invited to present our experience at the New York Academy of Sciences. The timing of the conference was a problem for me. During the next year, I would be in London on a Fellowship. I could not afford airfare.

I wrote to Harry on April 25, 1966, with virtual hat in hand. "I believe that I have a worthwhile contribution to make at the New York Academy meeting. I have a body of data on transsexuals that is unique. It consists of an assessment of 50 urologists, 50 gynecologists, 100 general practitioners, and 150 psychiatrists toward transsexualism and change-of-sex procedures. I have an unpublished compilation of specific objections by these physicians. Some are extraordinary and reveal naked irrational bias."

I was the third speaker:

"Physicians are rarely paralyzed by emotionalism in the management of their patients. The physician faced by a patient with severe heart disease or leukemia insulates himself from the spectre of death which consumes all men and administers what his training and judgment dictate as the treatment of choice."

"In one respect the patient with heart disease or leukemia is in an advantageous position. He is welcome in the physician's office; there are private foundations and public appropriations dedicated to administering to his needs. He is cradled by medicine, society, and his family. The transsexual is less fortunate."

"In our survey of American physicians, nine in ten psychiatrists objected to hormonal and surgical treatment on 'moral and/or religious grounds.' Most of the physicians would risk the patient's suicide rather than provide treatment." (6)

Before joining the Foundation, John Money had worked with surgeons at Johns Hopkins who had treated anatomically intersexed children, modifying their ambiguous genitalia to approximate the norm for their birth sex. One was a gynecologist, Howard Jones, Jr. and another, John Hoopes, a plastic surgeon. They were receptive to extending their work to adults. Our patient pool at the Foundation was the ideal source.

Ironically, at the time, surgical modification of an infant's genitalia was acceptable, but adult genital surgery was not. Today, that is reversed. There is considerable controversy over whether/when an intersex child, now termed a child with a disorder of sex development, should undergo surgical modification.

At a Benjamin Foundation meeting on December 10, 1965, I reported that Hopkins was to form a committee to consider cases for transsexual surgery. The Erickson Educational Foundation would underwrite some of the expense. With the committee in place, John Money introduced patients who had been extensively evaluated by the Foundation. Surgical treatments began.

Hopkins was not impatient to announce the program. There were concerns over publicity. But months later there was a leak in the *New York Daily News*, the tabloid that had broken the Christine Jorgensen story in 1952, about a sex-change operation at Hopkins. To put the best account forward, Hopkins issued a press release and sent it to the *New York Times*. It included, "If the mind cannot be changed to fit the body, then perhaps we should consider changing the body to fit the mind." On November 21, 1966 the front-page reported: "A Changing of Sex by Surgery Begun at Johns Hopkins." (7) With the prestigious Johns Hopkins Hospital as its medical sponsor, surgical treatment of the transsexual was legitimized.

TIME magazine quickly featured the Hopkins story. (8) Surprisingly, correspondence from readers was underwhelming. Fourteen letters were received, seven of approval.

The *American Journal of Psychiatry* published a harshly critical attack on the Hopkins program from a prominent psychiatrist, Joost Meerloo. (9) The *Journal* was not inundated with responses. There were two: both supportive of Hopkins—one was from me. (10)

An early outcry by a psychiatry professor was worthy of a bumper sticker:

COLLUSION WITH DELUSION

The venerable "unusual suspect", Charles Socarides, activated his cerebral short circuit to emit the predictable condemnation: "Such operations are doomed to cultivate failure because they do not change the basic underlying conflict." (11)

Janice Raymond denounced the procedures. She is described in Wikipedia as a "lesbian radical feminist activist". Sex-change was "to colonize feminist identity, culture, politics and sexuality. All transsexuals rape women's bodies by reducing the real female form to an artefact." (12) There you have it.

Paradoxically, religious leaders' reactions to the Hopkins program were more accepting. After the *New York Times* story, local Baltimore religious spokesmen were polled. There was striking support.

A Lutheran Church pastor: "Obviously this transsexualism is a mistake of nature and this surgery should be allowed." A Baptist minister: "If these people can be helped, Hopkins is proceeding in the right direction." The Dean of the Episcopal Cathedral: "The responsible use of surgical operations in such cases that cannot be corrected by psychotherapy would be in accord with Christian teaching." A rabbi: "I see this as purely a medical matter." Only the Catholic archdiocese withheld comment. (13)

A critical response from a Catholic priest was published later in a book on medical ethics: "…there can be no doubt on the immorality of the surgical procedures…the Principle of Totality imposes upon man to preserve bodily integrity. This must severely condemn surgery for transsexualism." (14)

A Talmudic scholar wrote to me and explained reservations and deliberations from a strict Jewish position. (On the one hand) "A normal male is under religious mandate to beget children. Both men and women are under strict commandment against unnecessarily endangering their lives. Surgical procedures involve serious dangers." (On the other hand) "If a group of reputable doctors would declare that the patient is in grave psychological state and that only the transsexual operation could restore him to mental health, then in such an extreme case the question might be reconsidered." (13)

(Decades later, a post-operative male-to-female transsexual was the official entry of Israel in the annual campy Eurovision Song Contest. All European countries vote for their favorite after a raucous televised evening of national presentations. Israel is an honorary country in Europe here (as it is in some sporting events) as their geographic neighbors will not accept them. When the Israeli entrant, Dana International, was voted the winner, a prominent Orthodox Israeli rabbi condemned the episode. But what did he know about music that is less than 5,000 years old?)

The Hopkins transsexual surgery program hit choppy waters years later, and then an iceberg. A new Department Chair was vehemently opposed to the surgery. Within the Department was a psychoanalyst who concocted a widely discredited study. I have used this study as a teaching example of how not to do research. It compared groups of patients, some of whom were surgically treated and some not, and found no better status in the surgically treated. The items on which the patients were rated were farcical. For example, the same score of minus one was given for a person arrested for a crime as someone who was cohabiting with a "non-gender-appropriate person". (15)

With this study as ammunition, the 1966 Hopkins program was closed in 1979. It would not reopen for thirty-eight years.

RICHARD RASKIND/RENEE RICHARDS

SEVENTEEN

MY GREEN DRESS

The large envelope I received in July 1967 contained a green dress and a packet of evangelical literature, along with a research questionnaire sent out three years earlier. The questionnaire was from our UCLA gender identity program and assessed physician attitudes toward sex change. While this respondent's attitude was clear, I did not understand the three-year delay.

Drawn up with Robert Stoller and psychologist Craig MacAndrew, the questionnaire had been sent to hundreds of psychiatrists, surgeons, and general practitioners. (1) We presented a case history of a typical male-to-female transsexual and the patient's request for hormonal and surgical treatments.

With no other information provided, nearly one in five physicians considered the patient to be psychotic (not surprising, as so little was known about these patients). But, surprisingly, six per cent of psychiatrists and twelve per cent of surgeons considered the patient a "threat to society". Less than ten per cent of physicians would agree to the requested treatments.

A stipulation was added that a psychiatrist found the patient not to be psychotic or severely mentally ill. Still, only a fifth of psychiatrists would endorse treatment and less than ten per cent of surgeons.

Then we added that the patient had undergone two years of psychotherapy, continued to want the treatments, and was judged by the psychiatrist to be reasonable in all other respects. Even then, only thirty per cent of psychiatrists would agree to the treatments and fewer than twenty per cent of surgeons. With the additional stipulation that the patient's psychiatrist endorsed surgery, still only a third of surgeons agreed, and a majority of psychiatrists refused.

The likelihood of the patient's suicide if treatment was refused had little effect on the groups' responses.

Reasons for disapproving were concern over having to explain their action to a medical society (four of five), a possible malpractice suit (two of three) and over nine in ten psychiatrists objected on "moral and/or religious grounds".

The outcry over this questionnaire nearly sealed my fate at UCLA. The Psychiatry head was swamped with protests over this questionnaire that offended many physicians. By then, I was out of the country in England on a fellowship. He vowed that I would not return to his department. Fortunately, he was antagonistic to others in the department as well and there was a coup d'etat. But the timing was problematic.

Bob Stoller wrote to me in London in June 1967, "It really is miserable that your career here has turned out to be dependent on the whim of the head's delaying his announcement and stepping aside, after the coup, and therefore not permitting the Department to reform and go on about its business. It is not possible for me to get you an appointment on the staff as long as he is still head. He is so specifically dead set against assisting you in your career that he has absolutely stood in its way." He was beheaded in time for me to return.

The physician who sent me the green dress in 1967 was not alone in a bizarre reaction to our questionnaire. One psychiatrist, revealing a hint of paranoia, demanded to know how his name had been selected to receive it. Another physician returned the questionnaire unanswered with multiple-choice options scrawled on the cover sheet:

Dr Green: If you have to select one answer, would you prefer to spit on A. The American Flag, B. The Bible, C. Your mother. If you don't get the message—forget it!

Until writing this, decades later, I did.

EIGHTEEN

THE GREEN MONEY BOOK

Surfing the crest of the wave of publicity over the 1966 Johns Hopkins surgical program for transsexuals, I planned to edit a scholarly text. It would be the first multi-disciplinary international collation. The logical publisher was the Johns Hopkins Press ("University" was not yet in their official title). John Money would be Advisory Editor.

In *How Sex Changed,* her excellent chronicle of transsexualism, historian Joanne Myerowitz characterized me as a professional tripod, with legs in three core circles. "Green had attended medical school at Johns Hopkins, where he worked with John Money on issues of crossgender identification in young boys, and in the early 1960s worked as a resident physician at UCLA with Robert Stoller. When he returned east in 1964, he began to collaborate with Harry Benjamin. He went to New York weekly to have dinner with Benjamin, see his patients, and attend meetings of his foundation. He also spent one evening a week working with Money in Baltimore. He kept Stoller apprised of the developments in New York and Baltimore. Green had the connections and credentials that enabled him to work easily with academics like Stoller and the offbeat personality that allowed him to fit in with Benjamin and his friends." (1) (Thanks, Joanne.) Perhaps this helped recruit contributors. Most were from UCLA, Johns Hopkins, and the Harry Benjamin Foundation.

At the outset of our text, John and I honored the "Father of Transsexualism". "The editors dedicate this book to Harry Benjamin, M.D., the pioneer of transsexual research. His compassion and courage in the treatment of the transsexual patient opened a new frontier in the knowledge of human nature." For a limited number of copies, the book contained a front piece full-page photo of Harry.

In the introduction, Harry wrote of seeing his first transsexual (referred by Alfred Kinsey in 1949). He described publishing the first medical article on transsexualism in 1953. He lamented that the medical profession treated these patients as "step-children". I have characterized them as "orphans".

Book preparation expenses of $2,200 were funded by the Erickson Foundation. It was repaid from royalties. In the foreword, Reed Erickson wrote from personal experience, "...where there was so much ignorance, there is now some real, detailed knowledge. Because of these achievements, a long-suffering human group now has a better chance to function satisfactorily. The transsexual's life was one of intense suffering fighting against feelings that were not only honest, but basic in the structure of personality. As this volume demonstrates, a courageous and skilled group has ventured into the unknown…to blaze a trail for understanding and faith."

Around that time, Reed and Harry had a falling out over several issues, some trivial. One was what color to repaint Harry's office. Funding to Harry's Foundation ceased. Then, over the years, Reed developed significant problems with drugs, notably cocaine. He was arrested more than once in the US. When he was holed up in Mexico, he experienced an acute drug-induced psychosis. John Money retrieved him for treatment at Hopkins. Reed protested that he had been kidnapped. He died in Mexico while a fugitive from American law enforcement.

In the preface I made it clear that the book was "not a forum for the many critics of sex reassignment to debate the controversial nature of these procedures. Considering the ample opportunity for critics of sex reassignment to express their view… the far more compelling need was for a scientific forum for the few scientists currently investigating transsexualism and sex reassignment."

Bob Stoller was the first to agree to contribute a chapter to *Transsexualism and Sex Reassignment*. He characterized the origins of transsexualism in the male from his lengthy psychoanalytic exploration in the mother of a femininely-identified young boy. Focussing on the relationship between the mother and young son, there was "excessive, blissful physical and emotional closeness between mother and infant, extended for years and uninterrupted by siblings. There had been strong transsexual tendencies in the mother throughout mid-childhood. The father was passive, scarcely at home during the child's first years and the marriage was empty and angry." In Bob's inimitable style, the excessive, symbiotic mother-infant son closeness yielded the mother's "feminized phallus".

Forty years later, at my UCLA memorial talk on Bob's classic 1968 *Sex and Gender,* I argued that his theory still needs to be tested. It is neither refuted nor confirmed. This because no clinical investigator has replicated Bob's research methodology. There has been no fashion for such in-depth investigation.

The "Green Money Book" provided an early opportunity to present the UCLA rationale behind our interactions with cross-gender boys and their parents. Working with Bob Stoller, I was interviewing adults pleading for sex change. Most were born male. It was mysterious how such an aberrant gender identity could evolve. Understanding this could illuminate the typical evolution of a core feature of human identity—I am male; I am female.

Clinical interviews of adult transsexuals about their childhood elicited an almost uniform response: "I have been this way all my life." They said they belonged to the other sex, and disliked dressing as, or doing things expected of, a child of their sex, but preferred the dress, activities, and companionship of persons of the other sex. Earlier work in my

Hopkins med school days with John Money suggested a research approach. We would find a group of boys with the behavioral syndrome or constellation of behaviors matching those recalled by adult transsexuals. We would record what they, and their parents, told us and arrange for periodic reassessment to observe the boys as they matured.

The parents who found us were concerned about their sons' behaviors. The boys were unhappy. They said they were, or wanted to be, girls, by words or actions. They were teased for their "sissy" behavior. At the time, there was more public attention given to the homosexual male than to the transsexual. Some parents were concerned about their boys becoming homosexual men. Stoller and I were focused primarily on pre-transsexuality. "What were transsexuals like as children? Could transsexuals be diagnosed during childhood? Could transsexuals be psychologically treated during childhood?" The title of the paper (co-authored with Bob and a child psychiatrist in our clinic, Larry Newman) expressed our understanding of the boys' behaviors and their implications: "Treatment of Boyhood 'Transsexualism'." (2)

Our clinical methods varied. Some families entered therapy, perhaps as small groups of parents and groups of children, or we talked individually with parents and children. Our view was that young children may see the gender world in black and white. A lack of interest in the popular activities of boys may lead the child to identify with the other sex. We encouraged parents to introduce other boys to their son who also were not athletes or rough-and-tumble, but were artistic, yet comfortable being boys. We found that father-son relationships were generally poor. Fathers had expected a son in tune with their masculine interests, such as sports. They were encouraged to engage in activities that both could find comfortable. Our goal was to reduce the gender pain in the child before it evolved to gender pain in the adolescent and adult.

My 1974 book on transsexual adults and "pre-transsexual" boys (published by Basic Books, Gerald Duckworth, and Penguin) (3) was *Sexual Identity Conflict in Children and Adults.* The follow-up text published in 1987 by Yale University Press was *The 'Sissy Boy Syndrome' and the Development of Homosexuality.* (4) The title demonstrated that the boys primarily became gay men, not women.

Some commentators objected that the title included "sissy boy". However, a gay anthropology professor told me that it captured perfectly how these boys behaved and the stigma they experienced for their constellation (syndrome) of behaviors that was a disorder according to the American Psychiatric Association and the World Heath Organization. Yale University Press initially objected because the title was not sufficiently academic. I suggested that they present an alternative. During the year that the book was in production, they did not.

For *Transsexualism and Sex Reassignment,* I had a scoop on English post-operative transsexuals. John Randall was the only clinician, other than Harry

Benjamin, who was assessing a large number of transsexual patients and endorsing some for hormonal and surgical treatment. I got to know him during my year in "swinging London" (1966). We often drank too much wine at his private club. He characterized transvestism as an obsession. Of this, he had personal knowledge, as noted in Section 21.

The results of twenty-nine male-to-female conversions under his guidance were mixed. Randall reported that seven were judged "excellent", fourteen "good", three "fair", and four were "poor". But surgery was primitive. Only eleven had a vagina constructed. Later research demonstrated that good reconstructive surgery was associated with better psychological adjustment. The female-to-male patients fared better, although penile construction was absent in most and primitive at best. Of six, three were judged "excellent", two "good" and one "fair." Nevertheless, "a majority of all patients are, in the end, content with their status. Certainly, there is often massive relief of mental suffering and discontent."

"Collusion with delusion" was the bumper sticker battle cry of opponents of sex reassignment medicine. In the text I countered, "The argument that sex-reassignment is collaboration with psychosis falters. There is no evidence from other psychiatric conditions demonstrating that fulfilling a patient's delusion results in psychiatric improvement."

I authored the "Green Money Book" conclusion. A half-century on, some comments remain topical.

On understanding a biological contribution to the development of transsexualism: "From the neuroendocrine approach, the eventual availability of measures of circulating gonadal hormones during prenatal development may provide a test with which to evaluate in man the significance of recent data pointing to the influence on postnatal behavior in animals." (Still waiting.)

On assessment of children: "An area of great practical as well as theoretic significance is research into childhood diagnosis and treatment of cross-gender behavior. The extent to which gender identity is malleable during childhood remains to be determined." (Currently an incendiary debate.)

Finally, "The research described in this text into the nature of an unusual human anomaly is consistent with the tradition of scientific inquiry and medicine—identify a basic phenomenon, understand underlying mechanisms, dispassionately assess methods of resolution, and in the process try to reduce human suffering. This is the essence of current interest in transsexualism and sex reassignment."

Over the months of book gestation, John's contribution increased. In a letter to the publisher in September 1967, I suggested that his title be upgraded to Associate Editor. At publication in 1968, John was co-editor.

The sale price of the 500-page "Green Money Book" was $15. At this writing, a new copy was listed on Amazon (only a river in 1968). Price: $2,500.

GREEN
AND
MONEY

TRANSSEXUALISM AND
SEX REASSIGNMENT

TRANSSEXUALISM AND
SEX REASSIGNMENT

EDITED BY
RICHARD GREEN, M.D. AND JOHN MONEY, PH.D.

NINETEEN

SLAM-DUNK SEX CHANGE

UCLA had not yet authorized a transsexual "sex-change" operation when I returned from my year-long fellowship in 1966 London. Enthused by my experience with transsexuals before London with Harry Benjamin, writing referrals for his patients to surgeons in Europe, I wanted UCLA to be part of this pioneering treatment.

To be safe, I needed a slam-dunk success patient to start with, or the program would sink. John Money had advanced the "Real Life Test" to predict post-surgery success. This was the period of time the candidate lived full-time in the desired gender role successfully, before surgery. One year was the minimum, with two preferred. (1)

I found the ideal patient. This male-born transsexual had lived as a woman for a decade. I presented Beverly to our Gender Identity Clinic at a Saturday morning conference in November 1968.

"We are going to see a twenty-five-year-old transsexual. This is a unique patient, one of the rare patients who fooled me when she called. On the phone, I did not suspect that she was transsexual. In person, I saw no clue either."

"As a child, this person reported that he was like a normal girl in play interests and wanting to dress as a girl. Parents thought their child would outgrow this phase. It continued in adolescence. Employment began in a cocktail lounge as a woman and she saved enough money to go see Harry Benjamin. Beverly told Harry she was eighteen when she was sixteen. He administered female hormones."

"Breast implants followed to enhance the hormone effect, and she had electrolysis for removal of facial hair. Her voice had not changed much at puberty. In the glee club she changed from a soprano to an alto."

"Beverly has been married as a woman for a year and a half. She was married in Reno and told them she had not brought her birth certificate but showed a drivers license with a woman's name and her photo."

Beverly was interviewed by Clinic members. She explained that she had not had genital surgery in all her years of living as a woman because she could not afford it. But Harry advised her to come see me at UCLA.

I was reassured by Bob Stoller on my selection for UCLA's first surgery. "If you could have a patient where it was inconceivable that she would get into any kind of psychological trouble, this would be the patient. If you are going to recommend the operation this is the kind of patient you're safer with than with any other."

For the surgical referral, I required a second psychiatric opinion. It was provided by Larry Newman, a UCLA psychiatrist and member of the Gender Identity Clinic. He wrote, "The patient is a tall, slim, entirely feminine 'woman'. Although I know for a fact, because of Dr. Green's statements and her own statements, that she is biologically male, there is nothing in her outward appearance to suggest that she is not a female. I can find no evidence to suggest that there is a psychiatric reason to deny her the procedure she is requesting. There is no psychiatric contraindication to the proposed sex-transformation surgery."

I referred Beverly to Will Goodwin, a urological surgeon who had previously been at Johns Hopkins. I informed Will that Beverly had been seen by me six times, by Dr. Newman twice, and had been favorably discussed at the Gender Identity Clinic. In my referral letter, I wrote "There is no evidence of psychosis or significant psychopathology outside of her anomalous gender identity. It is generally stated that such long-standing feminine identification is not amenable to change with psychotherapy."

Goodwin wrote to the medical school dean at UCLA, Sherm Mellinkoff (also an émigré from Hopkins). He stressed the technician role. "The position of the Division of Urology has been that when such a procedure is recommended to us, we will cooperate by carrying out the surgical procedure."

But there was another obstacle. Could sex-change surgery be mayhem? Mayhem is a criminal offense that originated from feudal England. It was used to punish anyone who cut off a limb from one of the king's fighting men to render him less capable in combat. From medieval law, it evolved into a statute in California. (2) I was advised of this and slowed our dash to the operating room. I consulted the Legal Counsel of the University of California. If I was going out on a limb to cut one off, I needed a legal net.

He replied that since we were trying to benefit the patient, and not trying to inflict harm, the sex change should not constitute mayhem. But, he could not be certain that we would not be prosecuted. If convicted, the penalty could be ten years in prison (in this case, fourteen, because it was a conspiracy between the surgeon and me). Reassuringly, the Legal Counsel added that if we were prosecuted the University would pay our legal fees.

The surgery went ahead. We were not prosecuted. Beverly did very well, socially and vocationally, living as a more complete woman. Slam-dunk.

TWENTY

MEDICINE FINDS ITS WAY: TREAT THE TRANSSEXUAL

With treatment of transsexuals becoming increasingly available, standardization of clinical care was required.

Eight of us founded the Harry Benjamin International Gender Dysphoria Association (HBIGDA) in 1978. There was Harry, of course, and three surgeons, a psychologist, a general practitioner, and a sex-reassigned teacher. A year later, five of us formulated what we believed to be the requisite standards of care for transsexual patients. It reflected our clinical experiences, and we hoped it would safeguard patients. (1)

Paul Walker, a psychologist in Texas who had worked with John Money, was chair. He was the first President of HBIGDA. Later he relocated to the hotbed of US gay life (San Francisco). We had a going-away luncheon for Paul a few years later as he neared the end of his short life, one of the seemingly unstoppable number of people destroyed by a rampaging virus.

In the Introduction to our *Standards of Care* we stated our rationale for these guidelines: "Forty centers in the Western Hemisphere offer surgical sex-reassignment to persons having a multiplicity of behavioral diagnoses, and are applied with various possibilities of care."

"Gender Dysphoria" was the description we applied to people requesting surgical and hormonal reassignment. (Thirty-five years later, the *Diagnostic and Statistical Manual 5 (DSM-5)* of the American Psychiatric Association replaced "transsexualism" with "gender dysphoria.")

We emphasized that hormonal and surgical sex reassignment "are not of such minor consequence to be performed on an elective basis." It was not to be provided "on demand". (This issue persists. Decades later, my patients at the government-funded Gender Identity Clinic in London resented that they had to see psychiatrists before they were allowed access to hormonal and surgical treatments. Clinic rules for treatment were based on our patient experience, and the politics of governmental funding. Patients we had seen seeking urgent reversal of surgery were those who bypassed the pre-surgical trial period of cross-gender living with psychiatric monitoring and sought foreign private fee surgeons. Public funding of a controversial treatment is more likely to continue if patients have undergone comprehensive medical assessment, rather than "treatment on demand").

Hormonal and surgical sex-reassignment was to be based on how well the patient fit the diagnostic criteria for transsexualism in the proposed American Psychiatric Association *Diagnostic and Statistical Manual III (DSM–III)* (with which I was also embroiled). Proposed criteria included a persistent sense of discomfort and inappropriateness about one's anatomic sex, and a wish to be rid of one's sex-identifying features and live as member of the other sex.

We recognized a problem with establishing the validity of a patient's reported life history of other-sex identity. Independent knowledge of the patient was required from family, or employer, or physician. The psychiatrist or psychologist recommending hormonal treatment should have known the patient for at least three months, and when recommending genital surgery, for at least six.

Our next provision became controversial three decades later when used by a private practice psychiatrist in London as a "diagnostic test" for transsexualism. It was "Hormonal sex reassignment is both therapeutic and diagnostic in that the patient either reports satisfaction or dissatisfaction regarding the results." His practice of too readily dispensing cross-sex hormones was challenged by other psychiatrists. It contributed to the clinician's censure by the General Medical Council (the United Kingdom medical registration and licensing body).

John Money's "Real Life Test" was considered to be the best indicator for progressing to surgical reassignment. It assessed "how successfully the patient has been living full-time, vocationally and avocationally, in all social situations and how successfully the patient has been in being accepted by others." The minimum period was twelve months.

The next two provisions remain controversial. "Hormonal sex-reassignment should be preceded by at least three months during which the patient lives full-time in the social role of the genetically other sex. Non-genital surgical reassignment (chest surgery) shall be preceded by at least six months." This was the treatment strategy of staged, fully reversible, before somewhat reversible, before irreversible procedures. Thus a social gender transition preceded hormonal intervention that preceded the ultimate surgery. The current *Standards of Care Version 7* permits hormone treatment when beginning social transition as well as breast surgery at that time. This change was in response to the difficulty females with large breasts were having concealing their breasts during the initial social transition. (2)

At the time, the *DSM-III* diagnostic proposal included the provision that the person's gender dysphoria not be symptomatic of another mental disorder, such as schizophrenia. There, a symptom of the disorder may be delusions of changing sex. This was addressed in our first version. The patient should be treated initially for the schizophrenia problems. Then, if the clinicians concluded that the person could be expected to benefit from sex reassignment, a diagnosis of schizophrenia would not preclude hormonal and surgical treatment.

Decades later at Charing Cross Hospital in London, I put this principle into effective practice. My patient had been experiencing schizophrenia problems for years. Unable to work, she lived in the community with social services support. She was convinced that doctors had implanted thousands of microplumbers in the blood vessels of her brain. She otherwise fit the criteria of an acceptable candidate for surgery. She was unhappy living as a man, and for years was more comfortable as a woman (albeit with the microplumbers). She had her surgery, and was more content (while still living with her guest plumbers).

Standards of Care 1 was eleven pages. *Version 7* is 112 pages. Treatment standards have been expanded to provide for those transgendered and requesting hormonal treatment, but not surgery, and those gender nonconforming, but not requesting medical treatments. (3)

In 1979, the currently controversial issues of treating adolescent transsexuals had not surfaced. We wrote, "Hormonal and surgical sex-reassignment may be conducted only with persons attaining their legal majority."

Attention is paid in the current version to the controversy over early childhood non-medical gender transition. For our first version, these were dimmer than specks on the horizon.

Terms to describe the new world of gender in the current version include "gender queer". In 1979, this would have raised a few eyebrows.

TWENTY-ONE

PSYCHIATRY FINDS ITS WAY: RECOGNIZE THE TRANSSEXUAL

It was time to prepare for the next version of the American Psychiatric Association's *Diagnostic and Statistical Manual of Mental Disorders (DSM-III)*. With me on the committee for *DSM-III* was Robert Stoller.

We introduced transsexualism. We described it in terms that had become standard from Harry Benjamin's earlier descriptions, and our UCLA clinical experience. There was to be a sense of discomfort and inappropriateness about one's anatomic sex, and a wish to be rid of one's sex-identifying features so as to live as a member of the other sex. This condition needed to be present for at least two years, and could not be a symptom of another mental illness. (1) *DSM-III* was published in 1980.

Legitimization of transsexualism as a medical psychiatric disorder did not open all doors to US insurance coverage. Some private companies barred the treatments. They were deemed "cosmetic", and therefore not insured. American state funding for low-income patients (Medicaid) was typically banned, as the treatment was considered "experimental". Federal funding for older patients (Medicare) was barred because treatments were judged "unsafe, experimental and controversial". (2) These funding bans were not reversed until 2014. (3)

In England, by contrast, the National Health Service had been providing treatment from the 1960s onwards. There was Charing Cross Hospital in London with John Randall as psychiatrist.

Randall was a careful clinician who assessed nearly as many gender dysphoric patients as Harry Benjamin. John became a friend in my 1966 London fellowship year. He had a home and family in North London. But he also had a flat in Central London. One evening, as we were preparing to go out for drinks and dinner at his club, he went to the wardrobe to get his coat. There were many dresses on hangers. "A woman stays here sometimes", he explained. I thought he had a mistress. I did not realize that they were his dresses.

Notwithstanding US insurance balking at funding care, with *DSM-III*, Harry Benjamin's medical orphans were adopted by the American Psychiatric Association.

TWENTY-TWO

GENDER COURT

TRANSSEXUAL TEACHERS

In 1974, a New Jersey teacher of ten year olds attempted to return to work after having transsexual treatment to live as a woman. The school refused. Testifying for the school was the usual "unusual suspect", Charles Socarides, who argued, "... the teacher functions as object for identification, and one of the major things in teaching is that we learn through identification with the teacher and very often we learn out of love for the teacher. And boys not only learn their lessons in school, they learn how to be men from their teachers. If such sexual change were known, it would be very disruptive of that process." (1) The teacher was barred because she was "incapacitated".

In 1979, I testified in court for another American teacher dismissed by a school board after having surgery to live as a woman. Experts for the school testified to the "grave, harmful psychological effects that the presence of the teacher would have upon many children who had formerly been the teacher's students while a male." I argued that this would not be harmful to students, but would be educative. The court ordered temporary reinstatement with back pay to be followed by a full administrative hearing. The teacher accepted a financial settlement, and the case did not proceed. (2)

TRANSSEXUAL PARENTS

In 1980, I was a court witness in the first case in England deciding whether a preoperative transsexual father living as a woman could have visitation access to a young daughter after divorce. I was invited to testify because three years earlier I had reported on families where sixteen children were being raised successfully by transsexual parents. (3)

The four year old girl was aware that the person dressing in women's clothes was also the person she had known as her father. One proposal before the court was that she would have no further contact with her father. This was to be explained by the falsehoods that he had died, or moved away too far to visit. I argued that she should continue contact during her father's gender transition. To assuage anxiety over a potential detrimental effect on the child, I suggested that she be seen by a mental health professional. I argued that the girl would be justifiably angered when she later learned that she had been lied to into believing that her father was unavailable.

The judge ruled that the father could be with the girl only when dressed in male-oriented attire, without jewellery or cosmetics. If, when visiting her, the father was "dressed in a way which was…aggressively feminine…it will be shown that his appreciation of the child's welfare was defective." This constraint was overruled on appeal. (4)

In another English case, the issue was whether a woman could have had sexual intercourse for years with a husband without being aware that the penis was a removable, artificial device. When the relationship failed, she argued in court that she had been unaware of the prosthetic penis and had been tricked into an illegitimate marriage because she believed the groom, born female, was male.

The case concerned the couple's adopted children (the apparent husband had acknowledged infertility). The mother did not want her former partner to have access to the children. She argued that he had not been a legal spouse and was not the children's biological father. My testimony emphasized the importance of psychological parenthood. The children had known this man as their father. He should not be divorced from their lives. We lost.

Also in England, another challenge for the transsexual family: when a male who fathers a child becomes a woman, should the child's birth certificate be amended designating the parent's name as a woman, and "father" changed to "parent"? I testified for a couple concerned that their children's birth certificate (indicating the parent's previous status as male) would be embarrassing to the child. It would reveal the parent as transsexual. The judge ruled against birth certificate change. If altered, it would interfere with the child's "right of respect for its private and family life to have its fundamental identity recognized. Such alteration may be adverse to the best interests of the child." (5)

NO "TIME OF THE MONTH" OBSTACLE
FOR THIS WOMAN PILOT

Kenneth Ulane, a four-year combat pilot veteran, and a twelve-year commercial pilot for Eastern Airlines (now defunct) in the US, took medical leave to undergo sex-reassignment surgery. She wanted to return as Karen Ulane. Eastern Airlines refused. As a gesture of "goodwill", they offered her a job in the airport flower shop.

I was an expert witness in federal court for Karen Ulane when she sued under anti-sex discrimination law. The attorneys argued that if this pilot was capable of flying as a man, but not as a woman, this was sex discrimination. (This seemed logical enough.)

The anti-sex discrimination law had an odd history. Usually, when a court attempts to understand the intent of a law, it looks to its history in the legislature before it was adopted. The problem here was that the sex-discrimination ban was part of a larger US proposed civil rights law to protect racial minorities. Opponents of that race protection law thought they would sabotage it by adding the sex discrimination section at the last minute. To their shock, the bill passed. So, there was no legislative history. (6)

On the witness stand, I began by educating the court on general matters of transsexualism. Then, when I was asked to describe the transsexual's sex after surgery, I laid out several criteria of sex: "psychological sex, chromosomal sex, hormonal sex, and appearance of the genitalia. If you look to chromosomes, they are male. If you look to the appearance of the external genitalia, they are female. If you look to hormonal sex, they would be female."

What then, the court asked, was Karen Ulane's gender? I answered, "Karen Ulane is a woman. Psychologically, she has a sexual identity of female, and behaves socially as a woman."

An expert witness for Eastern Airlines wrote the notorious article described earlier that maintained there was no benefit from transsexual surgery and helped close down the pioneering Johns Hopkins program. He testified that Ulane was not transsexual, but transvestic, a person with a more male identity. Therefore, the surgery was inappropriate. The pilot would be emotionally unstable. Airline passengers would be endangered.

The trial court ruled in our favor. It doubly did so. It held that Ulane was protected, not just from discrimination as a woman, but also from discrimination as a transsexual. In an astounding legal judgment and endorsement of Ulane, the judge wrote: "How much better a society is going to happen should Karen Ulane resume her seat in the cockpit.

It will happen with the help of people of good will like some who testified here in this courtroom."

The Court of Appeals disagreed. Barring her from returning as a pilot was not based on her being a woman, but because she was transsexual. The federal law was meant to prevent discrimination against men and women, not transsexuals. (7) It took me three years at Yale Law School after this trial to understand what that meant.

The bad outcome of the case remained "good law" (unmodified) for five years. Then, the Supreme Court held that sex discrimination law protects those who do not fit gender stereotypes. This would protect transsexuals. (8) By that time, I had graduated from law school.

Eight years after surgery, Karen Ulane died flying a vintage 1944 DC-3. She was instructing a co-pilot when the plane stalled and crashed.

A GHOST OF THIRTY YEARS PAST

This battle had been won decades ago (I thought). But word hadn't reached the North West Lancashire Health Authority in England. They authorize health care funds for their regional residents under the National Health Service. For their challenged administrators, transsexualism was not a medical disorder. Therefore, they did not have to provide treatment. Alternatively, if it was a disorder, the treatments with hormones and surgery were ineffective. But this was 1998, not 1966. Transsexual surgery was bundled with other non-fundable procedures such as correction of short-sightedness, hair transplants, and tattoo removal.

I endorsed three patients from that Health Authority funding area who had successfully negotiated the "Real Life Test" of trial cross-gender living and were suitable for surgery. Over the months, the Health Authority conceded that the patients might have a disorder. But the disorder was only a "condition", and not a "disease". Regardless, our proposed treatments were not "appropriate".

My twenty-five-page affidavit for the court included a compilation of positive treatment outcome studies from several countries. One was my review showing a ninety per cent reported success rate in hundreds of patients. (9) These studies were dismissed by the Health Authority because of possible bias in the medical reporting and the absence of randomized groups of non-operated patients (try signing up patients for this non-treatment group).

The Health Authority would only pay for counselling with the aim of promoting more comfort for patients living in their birth sex. But, as the Johns Hopkins press release of 1966 noted, after years of psychotherapists unsuccessfully trying to change these patients' minds, "If the mind cannot be made to fit the body, we should change the body to fit the mind."

A possible loophole for transsexual funding for a patient was an "overriding clinical need", or an "exceptional circumstance". This would occur if the patient had a serious mental illness. The serious illness, such as a psychosis, would have to result from the patient being denied sex change. But there were problems here. A severe mental illness developing during the "Real Life Test" of trial cross-gender living could be a disqualification for surgery. Further, the mental illness could be challenged by the Health Authority as deriving from denial of the requested treatment for transsexualism since that treatment was not considered appropriate. Catch-22.

The trial court ruled in favor of the three patients. It found that uniform denial of treatment was not permissible. (10) The Health Authority, reportedly trying to be frugal, could have quit and cut its potential losses. But it appealed the decision. The appeals court ruled that the Authority "does not in truth treat transsexualism as an illness, but as an attitude or state of mind which does not warrant medical treatment. The ostensible provision that it makes for exceptions in individual cases amounts to the operation of 'blanket policy' against funding treatment for the condition because it does not believe in such treatment." This was unlawful. (11)

For the money the Health Authority spent in court costs, it could have changed sex for half its residents.

TWENTY-THREE

BLOCK THAT PUBERTY?

The Standards of Care for Transsexuals, Version1 (co-authored by me in 1979) made no mention of gender dysphoric teenagers. But they were out there.

Transsexualism is usually not born full grown in adulthood. Most people in their early teens know if they want to change sex. Problematically, the physical changes of puberty are later obstacles to inconspicuous passing as a person in the new life role. This is especially visible in someone born male: facial hair, deep voice, height, Adam's apple.

Clinicians in the Netherlands, from the late 1990s, were putting puberty on hold for a year or so to give more breathing space to early teens to decide how to proceed. If they decided to continue with their birth sex, their innate puberty would be permitted to develop. If they wanted to live as a person of the other sex, they would receive hormones of the other sex. This was not allowed where I was in the UK.

In late Spring 2008, the Royal Society of Medicine (RSM) announced a day-long conference on adolescents with gender dysphoria. I thought they would address this emergent issue, and the UK out-of-step refusal to suspend puberty. But nowhere on the program were there clinicians who were blocking puberty. (1)

I contacted the program organizers, and argued for the inclusion of an expert from another country with a different approach. Too late. The program was full. But could they start the day-long event at 9:30 instead of 10, and make the coffee break a few minutes shorter to allow another speaker? Nope.

Angered, I decided to organize an alternative conference. (2) It was August. The RSM conference was set for late September. To land the first punch, I would hold it the day before the RSM meeting.

I had no speakers and no audience (of course, as no one knew about the plan). I had no funding. Fortunately, two UK charities were dedicated to transsexualism, one, in particular, to gender dysphoric children and teens. Both said they would provide seed money. I recruited speakers. The psychiatrist in Los Angeles who treated teens with sex hormones said he would come on an economy ticket. The expert in Boston said he would pay for his.

I needed happy consumers who had been treated with puberty blocking that was denied to UK teens. Two families would attend, one with a birth son (now daughter) one with a birth daughter (now son). They would be accompanied by their Dutch psychiatrist.

Then, a publicity breakthrough. A newspaper carried an article about *two* upcoming conferences. In an optimistic mood, I went to the local shop that printed my holiday cards and had them print a preliminary program. My "staff" arranged a conference site at Imperial College School of Medicine where I was a psychiatry professor.

Continuation training credits for attending conferences keep practicing clinicians practicing. The RSM paid staff arranged for their program to be granted five credits. My "staff" researched how to apply for education credits. Our conference was awarded six. Conference attendees for the day-long siege needed to eat. Lunch menus from Imperial College catering were created by the same dedicated "staff".

Now I needed an audience. With two weeks to go, there were fewer signups than speakers. Then a trickle. A small stream. Then a flood. The conference room was packed. My son had to run to a local sandwich shop for emergency food reinforcements.

Our conference was just before the RSM event. The Boston expert who presented at our conference was not at that meeting. During the final RSM discussion period, I announced why. "That clinician who is a leader in the treatment of young persons with gender dysphoria and who presented his experience at the Imperial College conference could not be here because he is an observant Jew. Today is the highest Jewish holy day. He returned to Boston to be with his family. With this scheduling precedent, perhaps RSM meetings next year will be on April 13 and September 12. The first is Good Friday. The second is the holiest day of Ramadan." A professor sitting next to me said, "They didn't like that."

A year later, the UK gender identity program announced that it would offer a medication to block puberty.

TWENTY-FOUR

TELEVISION EDUCATION: THE PUBLIC AS STUDENT

Testimony at a trial is heard by a dozen, a talk at a professional meeting is heard by a couple of hundred, a paper published in a professional journal is read by a thousand. But a TV appearance on *Oprah* is seen and heard by millions.

On US television, I discussed topics on sex and gender with Oprah Winfrey, Phil Donahue ("the thinking viewer's Oprah"), Ted Koppel, and lesser-known hosts from CNN, NBC, ABC and PBS and, in the UK, the BBC.

A 1991 *Nightline* broadcast by Ted Koppel achieved notoriety. Koppel had arrived at Syracuse University about the time I was leaving for Hopkins Medical School. He hosted *Nightline* for twenty-five years. A study had just been published showing a brain area size difference between homosexual and heterosexual men. The broadcast asked "Is Homosexuality

Biological?" Appearing with me were Evelyn Hooker and Jerry Falwell, as polarized a couple as could have been recruited.

Evelyn published the landmark study in 1957 (the year I left Syracuse and Koppel arrived) that launched research demonstrating that homosexuals were not mentally ill. She recruited dozens of homo-sexual men who were not in therapy and gave them psychological tests. She also tested heterosexual men not in therapy. She presented results to experts. No differences were found between the groups. (1)

Falwell was a pioneer televangelist. His view on homosexuality focussed on sin. He proclaimed that AIDS was God's punishment for homosexuals.

In the telecast, Evelyn and I endorsed the mental health of homosexuals and I suggested that if a biological basis was confirmed it could provide legal protection under American law. Falwell offered the prospect of redemption through change of sexual orientation.

Koppel asked, "Is it possible to cure a homosexual?"

I responded: **"The basic premise of your question implies disease. It is twenty years now since the American Psychiatric Association declared that homosexuality is not a disease."** Evelyn later told a reporter that she was "outraged" by Koppel's question, and described it as "monstrous".

Most of my mass-media television mini-lectures were in response to questions by the show's host. Sometimes I took questions from a studio audience.

A mother in one audience said she worried about her preschool son wanting to put on makeup and wear a dress. The host asked: "What should parents look for to assess whether their child is behaving as a normal boy or girl? Will this mother's child become gay or transsexual?"

I began: **"Parents can sometimes be concerned about the gender behaviors of a child that do not conform to those that are typical of boys or girls. There can be a relation between being a very feminine boy, and later being a homosexual man. In my fifteen year study about three-quarters of these boys matured as gay or bisexual, and one was transgender."**

I stressed: **"But there is a difference between children who do not conform to the cultural stereotypes of masculinity and femininity, and those with the psychiatric diagnosis of gender identity disorder. Many of these mature as gay. If they remain unhappy as boys or girls, as they mature into teenage, they may be transsexual, those who want to change sex."**

Another audience parent: "Can the behaviors be unlearned so the children become straight men?"

I replied: **"Some of the boys in my study were in therapy with a goal of more comfort being boys, and reducing cross-gender behaviors, and they became more conventionally masculine. But the per cent of those who became gay was the same as those who were not in any treatment."**

A host: "Are single mothers with no man in the home more likely to have homosexual sons?

I answered with research experience: "**No. I have worked with lesbian mothers who are raising their children alone or with a female partner. The gender identity of the children raised by lesbian mothers appears typical. They are content being boys or girls. Their boy-type and girl-type behaviors are conventional. So the likelihood is that the usual per cent, say ninety to ninety-five, will mature as heterosexual.**"

Another host: "Is there a difference between sex and gender?"

"**Sex is the biological insignia of male or female. Gender is how we relate as a man or as a woman with varying degrees of masculinity and femininity.**"

A host asked the big question that continues to motivate researchers: "How does this develop?"

"**To some extent we are trained and socialized in the first years to be masculine or feminine by name, clothes, toys. But it is not all socialization. Some of the differences can be related to influences before birth. Female children with a medical disorder in which, before birth, they produce excessive male hormone are more interested in some of the activities of boys. They are keener on rough-and-tumble play and sports.**"

"**We must look to the mix of nature and nurture. Very few things about us are purely genetic, such as eye color. And very few things are**"

purely learned, such as which language we begin speaking."

A studio guest, born male and living as a woman, reported that she would have female sexual partners after completing the transition. The host asked: "What does this mean?"

I explained: **"There was a theory that transsexual males were those who could not accept their homosexuality. So they became women to have sex with men. Now we see that we can separate sexual identity as male or female from sexual partner preference."**

A man in the audience, about thirty-five, volunteered that he had been cross-dressing since childhood and asked whether he would ever stop. "I still have the feeling that I'm a girl. Is there something wrong with me?"

I reassured: **"If you are conflicted about whether you are or should be a woman, there are experienced psychiatrists and psychologists to discuss this with."**

(I wondered how organizers for these daily TV shows found a man becoming a woman who would be lesbian and a man who worried all his life "that I'm a girl")

Another host: "What about the children of transsexual parents?"

I reported my research: **"I have seen about a dozen and a half. Their age range was 4-12, boys and girls. In none of them was there any conflict in terms of their own self-concept as male or female.**

In one family the mother became the legal father of four girls. All were conventionally feminine and heterosexual."

Another host with a core question: "What are the results of sex-change surgery?"

"The vast majority do very well if they have passed the "Real Life Test". This is one to two years living full-time before surgery in the life role they want. The treatment strategy is the most reversible procedure, such as clothing change, then hormone treatment, then surgery. The surgery should be the final anti-climactic step, not an enormous leap into womanhood or manhood."

After a host described a recent report of a brain difference between homosexual and heterosexual men, she asked for its significance.

"If homosexuality were demonstrated to be inborn, legally then, in American law, gays could have special protection from discrimination. Groups that are stigmatized and discriminated against for an inborn trait, such as race or national origin, that is unchangeable, are protected. If we can find that a specific part of the brain, as just reported, does differ then the discrimination may fall."

And the inevitable: "Can one take a homosexual and cause him to become heterosexual?"

"Essentially, no. Beginning with an exclusively homosexual person the most that might be accomplished is that you get some heterosexual behavior, but usually accompanied by homosexual fantasy.

The apparently heterosexual behavior of most people who show a change has been in those who were bisexual to begin with. So, the answer is no."

"The most important issue is coming to terms with who you are and making the best of who you are. It's not whether you love men or women—it's how you love. There are gays with problems. There are straights with problems."

My colleagues with families were a teaching lesson on mental health problems and sexual orientation. So, I added:

"I know a lot of psychiatrists supporting their kids through college by picking up the debris of heterosexual relationships."

TWENTY-FIVE

MY THREE KINGS

Apart from my dad who encouraged me to pursue my fascination with the 1952 headline "Ex-GI Becomes Blond Beauty", there were three others to whom I owe my career championing gay rights and honoring the need to live as a person of the other sex. They are my three kings.

John Money

John announced his innovative thinking in 1957, the year before we met. The dust jacket for his first book promised a "radical departure from established shibboleths". (1) That was only the beginning. In 2015, an edited book summarizing his controversial contributions to sexual science was called "Fuckology". (2)

John launched my career in gender and sex research when I was a first year medical student. We shared much early on and remained close for decades.

In my med school days, John was a patron of a young Baltimore artist, Lowell Nesbitt (later to achieve considerable prominence with some of his paintings featured on US postage stamps). On my wall are two Nesbitts from the 1950s, one based on an X-ray, and the other featuring an anatomy text illustration. John provided the images for both works.

An artist who John met through me in 1966, when I lived in London, was Yoko Ono. I had appeared in Yoko's film, *Bottoms*. It consisted of 100 performers' nude buttocks filmed while we walked individually on a rotating disc. When John was visiting me in London, Yoko was having one of her art installations at her flat in which viewers were asked to "progress the piece". The participant artist would drive nails further into a slab of wood or further smash chinaware. We visited and John contributed his artistic skill. In a few years, Yoko became world famous, carrying with her a touch of John.

In *Sexual Identity Conflict in Children and Adults* I wrote, "As a fledgling medical student in 1958, I was taken under the wing of a pioneering researcher. John Money provided encouragement to learn and reward for effort sufficient to motivate a commitment to psychological research when a myriad of career opportunities were being presented." (3)

John helped me name the journal I founded in 1971, *Archives* of *Sexual Behavior* and the sexual science organization I founded in 1974, the International Academy of Sex Research.

Robert Stoller

Although Robert Stoller was the only American academic (other than John Money) researching gender identity (a term Stoller coined), I had not heard of him when I applied for psychiatry training at UCLA. The attraction was the palm trees.

Bob adopted me in the way John had. In *Sexual Identity Conflict in Children and Adults*, I wrote, "Robert Stoller has provided the support, guidance, and unfailing confidence in me that set the course of my career." He wrote the book's foreword. (3) I was appointed Founding Editor of *Archives of Sexual Behavior*, thanks to Bob. He nominated me to the publisher.

Robert Stoller was the most honest of sexological reporters. He allowed us to see him naked. He published page after page of recorded therapy sessions. This was the unsterilized stuff of sexology. He published a five-hundred-page epic case report, much of it transcript, of a woman who believed she had a penis. (4) He complained, "Much of sex research wisdom is camouflaged by large samples, hidden in tabulated columns, and dissected beyond significance by statistical packages. Although statistical techniques may enable us to corroborate or deny a hypothesis, they do not produce one." (5)

Bob constantly refined his writings for clarity (to the dismay of our long-suffering, typewriter-bound secretary in the pre-computer era). He lamented, "I was innocent, and therefore optimistic to think that clarity was possible. Now I know that there is no such thing as a clear sentence. Maybe in a hundred years, sitting on my haunches like a Zen master, I shall finally write a clear sentence. But it will have no words." (6)

When Bob did use words, he had a wondrous way. I took one saying as an epigraph in my book *The 'Sissy Boy Syndrome' and the Development of Homosexuality*: "Artists lie to tell the truth, and scientists tell the truth to lie."

When it came to sex-change surgery, Bob was sympathetic, remarkable for a psychoanalyst. Here was the antithesis of treatment for castration anxiety--castration. He encouraged me to promote the first transsexual operation at UCLA. But he was not entirely convinced of the success of "sex-change" for a person born male. He characterized the post-op patient as a "Near Miss".

Robert Stoller was killed in his car by a speeding driver. A few days earlier, I had received an ominous medical report on a lesion in my liver. There were three diagnostic possibilities--the two more likely were terminal malignancies. Immediately, I went to his office for comfort. I told him that I would have a more sophisticated confirmatory test in two days and, if the result was bad, I would need him emotionally. He nodded, silently. That was the last time I saw him.

When my medical test confirmed the third, benign, diagnosis, Bob had already left UCLA. I left a message on his home answering machine that everything was OK. He got the message. Then he drove off. In a couple of minutes he was dead.

Harry Benjamin

I was introduced to Harry Benjamin by John Money in 1964. Harry was relatively young then, about seventy-nine. He would live to be one hundred one-and-a-half.

Harry had no children. So, when it came time to retire, he wanted a young physician to take over the "family business". I declined. I wanted to be an academic. But we remained in close contact. He would telephone me in Los Angeles every Sunday. I would visit him in the summer in San Francisco where he had his second office. Later, when I was at the university in Stony Brook, New York, I would visit Harry in his Manhattan apartment. He would be listening to the opera. He would always have news clippings on transsexualism to share.

I attended Harry's 100th birthday party. I spoke at his memorial a year and a half later.

"This was Harry's third half-century. What Harry achieved in his second half-century exceeded what the most successful of mortals accomplish in their first. The "Father of Transsexualism" did not see his first transsexual until the age when most of us retire."

"Harry and I would eat dinner Saturday evenings in a small Swiss restaurant. He regaled me with his unique experiences. He told me of his interview with Freud. He revealed Freud's secret that he had undergone an operation to restore sexual vigor. At another time, Harry was the star-stuck opera fan when revealing how he examined Caruso's vocal cords."

"Harry's compassion and affection for every patient, and his heroism in the face of scorn, lives within those who honor him today, and tomorrow."

Other speakers included tennis star Renee Richards and John Money. Recently, I watched a tape of those presentations from decades ago. We were all so young then. Except Harry.

In a small way, I have been able to pay back my three kings.

My opportunity with John was in two parts.

John finished writing his first-person history of the development of the discipline of pediatric psychoendocrinology (the interrelation between hormones and behavior in children). It was rejected by an editor because it was "too autobiographical". This misguided expert had dismissed its unique value. I arranged to publish it in my edited series on sexuality. (7)

In 2004, the British Broadcasting Company (BBC) produced a television documentary on the controversial male twin case in which one had been raised as a girl from early childhood, at John's advice. This was after the young boy's penis was destroyed in a circumcision mishap. The documentary, rich with the wisdom of hindsight after the sex reassignment failed, was a hatchet job against John. I was John's sole defender. I said, "Based on what was known at the time about how you become a boy or a girl, and knowing the difficulties of creating a penis surgically, the decision that John Money made was the correct one."(8)

My opportunity to repay Bob came after his death. It was like discovering a previously unknown recording by the Beatles. Two months before the car crash, Bob had finished the book *Sweet Dreams: Erotic Plots*. It was placed in a publishing queue by his retiring editor. But then the publisher decided to discontinue works by psychoanalysts.

In a 2007 visit to his widow, Sybil, she showed me the manuscript. For a decade and a half, Bob's final book languished on a shelf. When I returned to London, I gave it to Karnac Books, one of the last psychoanalytic publishers still standing. A bonus book by Bob. (9)

My opportunity to repay Harry also came after his death. The professional association I co-founded in 1978 honoring Harry's work with transsexuals was the Harry Benjamin International Gender Dysphoria Association. In 2006, Association officers decided to change its name. "Harry Benjamin" was to be dropped from the title. An argument for erasing his name was that young members did not know who he was. Exactly the reason to retain the original name! I forced the officers to put the decision to a membership vote. Harry and I lost.

My three kings were very different.

One was born in Germany (Harry), one in New Zealand (John), and one in the US (Bob). One was very wealthy, living on a multi-acre secluded estate, with a stable, a wine cave, a pool, and live-in servants

(Bob). One was middle-class, living in an antique-decorated city apartment (Harry). One lived frugally, in an urban ghetto crammed with West African, Maori, and other pacific region artefacts (John). One was monogamously heterosexual, with four sons (Bob), one was married to a woman decades his junior, and childless (Harry), and one was childless, bisexual, and a libertine (John).

They shared two things in common. The first was their unprecedented understanding and compassion for gender and sexual development and expression. The second was confidence in me.

After my father, these were my three kings.

JOHN MONEY

BOB STOLLER

HARRY BENJAMIN

TWENTY-SIX

AFTERWORDS: THE TIMES THEY ARE A-CHANGIN'

"Come senators, congressmen
Please heed the call
For the times they are a-changin' " (1)

Employment

In the four decades following the 1950s, the US government fired employees if revealed as homosexual or would not hire (along with "other sex perverts"). They were regarded as blackmail bait who compromised national security. (2)

Then, in 1995, a federal breakthrough. President Clinton declared, "The United States Government does not discriminate on the basis of sexual orientation in granting access to classified information." (3) But it was 2015 before federal government employ-

183

ees were protected from other types of discrimination based on gender identity or sexual orientation.

Each year, since 1994, there has been introduced into the US Congress a bill to ban employment discrimination at the national level by private employers based on sexual orientation and, in some years, also gender identity. It is the "Employment Non-Discrimination Act". It has never passed. (4)

At the state level, Pennsylvania was the first to ban public sector employment discrimination based on sexual orientation. This was in 1975. Wisconsin followed seven years later. In another year, Minnesota included gender identity. (5) Still, fewer than two dozen states protect sexual orientation and gender identity in public and private employment by statute. Some others have executive orders by the governor. Sixteen states provide no protection. (6)

In the United Kingdom (UK), the Equality Act 2010 makes it unlawful to discriminate against employees or job seekers because of their sexual orientation. (7)

Homosexuality and the Military

Under President Truman, the Uniform Code of Military Justice of 1950 forbade sodomy, characterized as "unnatural carnal copulation with the same or opposite sex or with an animal." (8)

Over the decades, acceptance of homosexual Americans serving in the military fluctuated. During times of crisis, sexual orientation went out of focus.

Homosexual volunteers and draftees entered to bolster military ranks. When a crisis subsided, stricter scrutiny returned.

For a time, a single homosexual act was not grounds for discharge from the military. It was a "one-off" and colloquially known as the "Queen for a Day" defense, adapted from the name of a television show of the time. Yet, annually, thousands were "dishonorably" discharged. After WWII, the dishonorably discharged were ineligible for the GI Bill of benefits that funded access to education. (9) For many years, inclusion of "dishonorably discharged" was a stain on applications for employment.

Then, as other Western nations successfully integrated homosexual men and women into their military, the US Department of Defense came under pressure. In his first run for the presidency, Clinton promised "to reverse the ban on gays and lesbians." But, after his election, strong congressional opposition resulted in a partial climb-down. He instigated "Don't Ask, Don't Tell" (DADT). His compromize "ceded substantial concessions to the military and delivered a significant blow to gay rights advocates." (10) Under DADT, a service person could not be asked to reveal their sexual orientation, was not to voluntarily reveal it, but also could not engage in a homosexual act. An act included holding hands. DADT operated from 1993. (11) Under this policy, 12,000 were discharged. A federal appeals court suspended DADT in 2010 after lower court rulings that it violated free speech. President Obama signed the DADT Repeal Act of 2010. (12)

In the UK, sexual orientation was not a barrier from 1999. The government was dragged into accommodation by a ruling of the European Court of Human Rights. (13) Now the British military recruits gay men and lesbian women at Gay Pride events.

Gender Identity and the Military

The US military barred transsexual applicants. "Genital defect" was a physical disability, and it included penile amputation or a major abnormality of the genitals as would occur with a change of sex. (14) This policy, too, gradually generated opposition. In 2015, the American Medical Association approved a resolution against the ban.

By 2016, European countries, including France, Germany, Spain, Belgium, Sweden, and Austria accepted transgender military personnel. The RAND Corporation (an American think tank) studied its impact on the armed forces in Australia, Canada, the UK, and Israel. No detrimental effect was found on operational effectiveness, readiness, or group cohesion. (15)

In his final year as president, Obama proposed a policy whereby a US military person could no longer be discharged, or denied reenlistment, for being transgendered. Dozens of military personnel petitioned for transsexual surgery. (16) Just before its implementation, newly-elected President Trump reversed the directive. "After consultation with my generals and military experts, the United States Government will not accept or allow transgender individuals in any capacity in the US Military. Our military must be focussed on decisive and overwhelming victory, which cannot be burdened with the tremendous medical costs and disruption that transgender in the military would entail." (17) The reversal was suspended by federal court judges in late 2017, pending a final court review. In early 2018, transgender military personnel remained in service and recruits were processed, subject to stringent appraisal for medical and psychological stability.

Transsexual veterans have always been barred from surgery under the otherwise comprehensive US government health care program for ex-military personnel.

Early in the Obama administration, a closeted transsexual soldier, Bradley Manning, leaked thousands of classified federal documents to the internet source, Wikileaks. Manning was sentenced to thirty-five years in federal prison. Shortly after incarceration, Manning announced that henceforth she was to be known by her woman's name, Chelsea. Nevertheless, Manning continued to be kept in a male prison. As one of his last presidential acts, Obama commuted the remaining years of Manning's sentence. (18)

The UK has accommodated transgender military personnel since 1999. "The Army welcomes transgender personnel, and ensures that all who apply to join are considered for service, subject to meeting the same mental and physical entry standard as any other candidate." If the candidate has completed gender transition, enrolment is in the "acquired gender". (19)

Age and Gender Dysphoria

Our brave new world of treating adults with gender dysphoria in the office of Dr. Harry Benjamin in the 1960s became mundane. A few decades later, the controversy engaged adolescents, first in mid-teens, and then just entering puberty. Would mid-teens receive cross-sex hormones? Would those just entering teens have unwanted puberty blocked?

Now, turmoil focuses on gender dysphoric young children well before puberty. Should they have a non-medical transition to live socially as a child of the other gender? A US reality television show follows one child who transitioned at age four into teen years. (20) The January 2017 cover of *National Geographic* magazine displayed a transitioned child.

Today's braver new world was invisible to us as we raised our heads above the parapet in Harry's office a half-century ago.

Public Opinion

Sex

In 1974, when I argued on American television for same-sex marriage, it was supported by fewer than one in ten Americans. Now it is supported by a majority. In the UK it is approved by two in three.

In 1978, I argued in print for gays and lesbians being able to adopt children. This was also supported by fewer than one in ten in the US and Britain. Now it is supported by a majority.

Forty years ago, over half of Americans viewed homosexuals unfavorably. Two in three considered homosexuality "always wrong" and a "sin". Now the majority are accepting. In the UK, two in three had considered it to be "morally wrong". This is down to one in five.

Gender

When we polled American physicians on their attitudes toward transsexuals in the mid-1960s, most would have condemned the person to a likely suicide rather than grant the requested treatments. The general public had essentially no view, as there was little attention to these desperate persons. Concern increased in later decades, and "T" was added to the advocacy movement that had championed lesbian, gay, and bisexual rights to form LGBT.

In the US, three in four now agree that the legal protections that apply to gays and lesbians should also apply to the transgendered. (21-26)

In the UK, the majority approve of medical treatment for transsexuals, although most do not favor it being paid for by the financially-beleaguered government health service.

This half-century of revolution, proceeding with small evolutionary steps, reflects a profound understanding of two of the most fundamental features defining personhood-- sex and gender.

"For the loser now
Will be later to win
For the times they are a-changin' " (1)

TWO

1. Leviticus Chapter 20, verse 13.
2. Buggery Act 1533. 25 Henry 8, C.6
3. Paragraph 143, Prussian Penal Code and Its Maintenance and Paragraph 152, Draft Penal Code, North German Confederation.
4. Krafft-Ebing, R. von 1898. *Psychopathia Sexualis.* Stuttgart, Ferdinand Enke.
5. Bentham, J. 1785. *Offences Against One's Self: Paederasty.* Available 1978, Journal of Homosexuality 3:389-405.
6. Crompton, L. 1976. Homosexuals and the Death Penalty in Colonial America. University of Nebraska-Lincoln.
7. Fitzpatrick, J. Editor. 1934. *The Writings of George Washington from the Original Manuscript Sources 1745-1799, Vol.11.* United States Government Printing Office.
8. http://www.executedtoday.com/2013/02/01/1816. Africaine-Sodomy/

9. American Psychiatric Association 1952. *Diagnostic and Statistical Manual of Mental Disorders.* Washington, Author.

10. Employment of Homosexuals and Other Sex Perverts in Government. Document 241, interim report, Senate Subcommittee of Investigations, 81st Congress, 2d Session.

11. Bullough, V. 2002. *Before Stonewall: Activists for Gay and Lesbian Rights.* New York, Haworth.

12. American Law Institute Model Penal Code 213.2 (Recommendation 1955, Proposed Official Draft 1962).

13. Rutledge, L. 1972. *Gay Decades*, p.46. New York, Plume.

14. hansard.millbanksystems.com Sexual Offences (No.2) 5 July 1966.

15. Tatchell, P. 2017. Fifty years of gay liberation? *The Guardian* 23 May, p. 31.

16. Lisker, J. 1969. Homo Nest Raided, Queen Bees Are Stinging Mad. *New York Daily News*, July 6.

17. todayinclh.com/event-first-gay-liberation-day

18. Freud, S. 1935. Letter to an American Mother. Reprinted in *American Journal of Psychiatry* 1951, 107:786-7.

THREE

1. Green, R. and Money, J. 1960. Incongruous gender role: non-genital manifestations in prepubertal boys. *Journal of Nervous and Mental Disease* 131: 160-68.

2. Green, R. and Money, J. 1961. Effeminacy in pre-pubertal boys: summary of eleven cases and recommendations for case management. *Pediatrics* 27: 286-91.
3. Hoffman, M. 1968. *The Gay World.* New York, Basic Books.
4. Green, R. 1981. Martin Hoffman: A Memory. *Archives of Sexual Behavior* 10:549-550.

FOUR

1. Green, R. 1972. Homosexuality as a mental illness. *International Journal of Psychiatry* 10:77-98.
2. Kinsey, A., Pomeroy, W., and Martin, C. 1948. *Sexual Behavior in the Human Male.* Philadelphia, W.B. Saunders.
3. Ford, C. and Beach, F. 1951. *Patterns of Sexual Behavior.* New York, Harper.

FIVE

1. Freud, S. 1921. Letter (to Ernst Jones). Body Politic, May 1977, p. 9.
2. Bieber, I. et al. *Homosexuality: A Psychoanalytic Study.* New York, Basic Books.
3. Green, R. 1987. *The 'Sissy Boy Syndrome" and the Development of Homosexuality.* New Haven, Yale University Press.

SIX

1. Bayer, R. 1981. *Homosexuality and American Psychiatry*. New York, Basic Books.
2. McConahy, N. 1976. Is a homosexual orientation irreversible? *British Journal of Psychiatry* 129:556-63.
3. https://www.wired.com/2016/11/dr_h_anonymous./
4. Stoller, R. et al. 1973. Should homosexuality be in the APA nomenclature? *American Journal of Psychiatry* 130:1207-16.
5. BBC News. 25 August 2006. Pluto vote 'hijacked' in revolt.
6. Lesse, S. (1974). To be or not to be an illness. *American Journal of Psychotherapy* 28:1-3.
7. Socarides, C. 1992. Sexual Politics and Scientific Logic: The Issue of Homosexuality. New York, Association for Psychohistory.
8. American Psychiatric Association. 1980. *Diagnostic and Statistical Manual of Mental Disorders III*. Washington, Author.
9. Brody, J. 1982. Psychiatrists on Homosexuality: Vigorous Discord Voiced at Meeting. *New York Times*, January 26.
10. American Psychiatric Association. 1987. *Diagnostic and Statistical Manual of Mental Disorders III* R. Washington, Author.
11. Green, R. 1986. Letters to the Editor. *Psychiatric News*. September 19.

SEVEN

1. Holland v Holland, 75 N.E. 2d 489 (Ohio, 1947)
2. Immerman v Immerman, 176 Cal App 2d 122 (1959)
3. Chaffin v Frye, 45 Cal.App.3d 39 (1975)
4. Townend v Townend No. 74 CV0670 County Common Pleas. Portage County, Ohio. April 4, 1975.
5. Townend v Townend, No. 639 County of Portage, Court of Appeals, Ohio. September 30, 1976, p. 3.
6. Schuster v Schuster and Isaacson v Isaacson, No. D36868, 36867. Superior Court, State of Washington, King County 1974.
7. Schuster v Schuster 585 P.2d 130 (Wash 1978)
8. In re J.S.andC. 324 A.2d 90, Superior Court N.J. (1974) aff'd 362 A.2d 54 (1976)
9. Peterson v Peterson, No. D-66634, District Court of Denver, State of Colorado. April 24, 1978.
10. Haney-Caron, I. and Heilbrun, K 2014. Lesbian and gay parents and determination of child custody: the changing legal landscape and implications for policy and practice. *Psychology of Sexual Orientation and Gender Diversity* 1:19-29.

EIGHT

1. MLA: Advocates: Should Marriage Between Homosexuals be Permitted? 05/02/1974 WGBH

Medical Library &Archives, http://openvault.
wgbh.org/catalog/v-57993D38129A433AAD10
C7BO4DO19EF6>

2. American Enterprise Institute. www.aei.org
3. Article IV, section 1
4. 1 U.S.C. Section 7 and 28 U.S.C. 1738C
5. US v Windsor 570 US 744 (2013).

NINE

1. The Immigration Act of 1917 (Chapter 29, Section 3, 39 statutes 874.
2. Draper, G. 1939. Mental abnormality in relation to crime. *American Journal of Medical Jurisprudence 2:161.*
3. La Rochelle, 1965. 11 Immigration and Naturalization 436.
4. Senate Report 1137, 82d Congress, 2d Session 1952.
5. 57 Interpreter Releases 440, 1980.
6. Public Health Service, Report on the Medical Aspects of HR 2379, in HR Rep. 1365, 82d Congress, 2d Session 1701, 1952.
7. House of Representatives No. 1365, 82d Congress, 2d Session, 46-48, 1952.
8. Morales v. United States. Report of Justice Immigration Court. File A12 796 782 August 15, 1980.

TEN

1. Green, R. 1978. Should Homosexuals Adopt Children? The Burden Is On Those Who Say No. In *Controversy in Psychiatry,* Brady, J, and Brodie, H. eds. pp 813-28. Philadelphia, W.B. Saunders.
2. www.gallup.com/poll/9916/Homosexuality.aspx
3. Green, R. Mandel, J. Hotvedt, M., Gray, J. and Smith, L. 1986. Lesbian mothers and their children: a comparison with solo parent heterosexual mothers and their children. *Archives of Sexual Behavior* 15:162-84.
4. Bayer, R. 1981. *Homosexuality and American Psychiatry.* New York, Basic Books.
5. Gonsiorick, J. 1982. Results of psychological testing on homosexual populations. *American Behavioral Scientist* 25:385-96.
6. In re Adoption of X. X. G. Third District Court of Appeals, Florida (2010)

ELEVEN

1. Wolinsky, M. and Sherrill, K. editors. 1993. *Gays and the Military.* Princeton, Princeton University Press.
2. History of US Military's Policy on Homosexuals. The Boston Globe.boston.com
3. Green, R. 1993. On Homosexual Orientation as an Immutable Characteristic. In *Gays and the*

Military, Affadavit I, pp.56-83 and Affidavit II, pp. 171-73.

4. McConahy, N. 1976. Is a homosexual orientation irreversible? *British Journal of Psychiatry* 129:556-63.

5. Green, R. 1987. *The "Sissy Boy Syndrome" and the Development of Homosexuality*. New Haven, Yale University Press.

6. LeVay, S. 1991. A difference in hypothalamic structure between heterosexual and homosexual men. *Science* 253:1034-7.

7. Steffan v Cheney 733 F. Supp 121, Court of Appeals, District of Columbia Circuit (1989)

8. Jackson, R. 1991. Lawyers Cite Sexual Slur. *Los Angeles Times*, March 10.

9. Steffan v Cheney 920 F.2d 74 Court of Appeals District of Columbia Circuit (1990).

10. Naval Aviation Foundation. US District Court of Appeals for the District of Columbia Circuit. Steffan v Aspin, No. 91-5409.

11. Steffan v Aspin. US District Court of Appeals for the District of Columbia Circuit (1993)

12. Steffan v Aspin. 8 F.3d 57, US Court Court of Appeals, District of Columbia Circuit.

13. House of Representatives repeals "Don't Ask, Don't Tell," Bill 2965, Senate repeals "Don't Ask Don't Tell," Bill 4023.

TWELVE

1. On my honor I will do my best,
   To do my duty to God and my country and to obey the Scout Law
   To help other people at all times
   To keep myself physically strong, mentally awake and morally straight.
2. Curran v Mount Diablo Council of Boy Scouts of America. 147 Cal. App. 3d 712 (1983).
3. California Civil Code. Section 51 (1959).
4. Harris v Capital Growth Investors XIV 52 Cal. 31, 1142 (1991).
5. Bayer, R, 1981. *Homosexuality and American Psychiatry*. New York, Basic Books.
6. Curran v Mt Diablo Council. Superior Court Decisions of November 6, 1990 and May 21, 1991.
7. Curran v Mt Diablo Council. Court of Appeal. March 29, 1994
8. 17 Cal. 4th 670 (1998)
9. Brown, J. 17 Cal. 4th 670 (1998) concurring opinion.
10. Boy Scouts of America v Dale 530 US 640 (2000).
11. *National Catholic Register*. Boy Scouts of America Lifts Ban on Homosexual Scouts. May 2013.

THIRTEEN

1. Fejes, F. 2008. *Gay Rights and Moral Panic.* New York, Palgrave MacMillan.
2. Bayer, R. 1981. *Homosexuality and American Psychiatry.* New York, Basic Books.
3. Bryant, A. and Green, B. 1978. *At Any Cost.* Grand Rapids, Fleming H. Revell.
4. Voeller, B, 1979. My Days on the Task Force. Christopher Street, October, p. 63.
5. Psychiatrists, Clergy Speak Out on Gays. 1977. *Miami Herald,* June 4.
6. Bryant, A. 1978. *PLAYBOY.* November.
7. Navarrro, M. 1998. 2 Decades On Miami Endorses Gay Rights. *New York Times,* December 2.

FOURTEEN

1. What America Thinks. National Opinion Research Center at University of Chicago. October 1966.
2. Colorado Constitution Article II, Section 30b.
3. Keen. L. and Goldberg. S. 1998. *Strangers to the Law.* Ann Arbor, University of Michigan.
4. Evans v Romer 854 P.2d 1270 (Colo.1993) and 882 P.2d 1335 (Colo.1994).
5. Keen L. and Goldberg, S. 1998. *Strangers to the Law.* Ann Arbor, University of Michigan, p. 47
6. Weinrich, J. 2016. Personal communication.

7. Bailey, J. and Zucker, K. 1994. Childhood sex-typed behavior and sexual orientation. *Developmental Psychology* 31:43-55.

8. *Denver Post.* 1993. October 13. p. 8A.

9. Pankvatz, H. 1993. *Denver Post.* October 14, p. 1B.

10. American Psychological Association 1983. Letter from American Psychological Association to Paul Cameron dropping him from membership. December 2. http://psychology.ucdavis.edu/rainbow/html/Cameron_apaletter.html

11. American Sociological Association 1987. Official Reports and Proceedings. Footnotes 15 (2):14.

12. Socarides, R. 1996. *Washington Blade*, April 22.

13. Romer v Evans 517 US 620, 1996.

14. Senate Bill 25. 2007. Sexual Orientation Workplace Discrimination.

FIFTEEN

1. Ex-GI Becomes Blond Beauty. 1952. *New York Daily News*, December 1.

2. Meyerowitz, J. 2002. *How Sex Changed.* Cambridge, MA. Harvard University Press. p.283.

SIXTEEN

1. Richards, R. with Ames, J. 1983. *Second Serve.* New York, Stein and Day.

2. Green, R. 1966. Appendix C in Benjamin, H. *The Transsexual Phenomenon.* New York, Julian Press.

3. Guze, H. 1969. Psychosocial Adjustment of Transsexuals. In *Transsexualism and Sex Reassignment*. Green, R. and Money, J. editors. p. 171. Baltimore, The Johns Hopkins Press.

4. Doorbar, R. 1969. Psychological Testing of Male Transsexuals. In *Transsexualism and Sex Reassignment*. Green, R. and Money, J, editors. p. 189. Baltimore, The Johns Hopkins Press.

5. Hellman, R., Green, R., Gray, J. and Williams, K. 1981. Childhood sexual identity, childhood religiosity, and homophobia as influences in development of transsexuals, homosexuals, and heterosexuals. *Archives of General Psychiatry* 38:910-15.

6. Green, R. 1967. *Transactions of the New York Academy of Sciences* 29: 428.

7. Buckley, T. 1966. A Changing of Sex by Surgery Begun at Johns Hopkins. *New York Times* p. 1, November 21.

8. *TIME*, 1966, Medicine Section, December.

9. Meerloo, J. 1967. Change of sex and collaboration with the psychosis. *American Journal of Psychiatry* 124:263-4.

10. Green, R. 1968. Letter to the Editor. *American Journal of Psychiatry* 124: 997- 8.

11. Socarides, C. 1966. *Newsweek*, A Change of Gender, December 5, p.73.

12. Raymond, J. 1979. *The Transsexual Empire*. Boston, Beacon Press.

13. Green, R. 1969. Attitudes toward transsexualism and sex reassignment. In *Transsexualism and Sex*

Reassignment, Green, R. and Money, J. editors. p. 235. Baltimore, The Johns Hopkins Press.

14. McFadden, C. 1967. *Medical Ethics* 6ed. p. 283, Philadelphia, Davis.

15. Meyer, J. and Reter, D. 1979. Sex reassignment: follow-up. *Archives of General Psychiatry* 36: 1010-15.

SEVENTEEN

1. Green, R., Stoller, R. and MacAndrew, C. 1966. Attitudes toward sex transformation procedures. *Archives of General Psychiatry* 15: 178-82.

EIGHTEEN

1. Myerowitz, J. *How Sex Changed.* Cambridge, MA. Harvard University Press. p. 223.

2. Green, R., Newman, L. and Stoller, R. 1972. Treatment of boyhood "transsexualism". *Archives of General Psychiatry* 26:213-7.

3. Green, R. 1974. *Sexual Identity Conflict in Children and Adults.* New York, Basic Books; London, Gerald Duckworth; Baltimore, Penguin.

4. Green, R. 1987. *The 'Sissy Boy Syndrome' and the Development of Homosexuality.* New Haven, Yale University Press.

NINETEEN

1. *Standards of Care, Version 1.* 1979. Harry Benjamin International Gender Dysphoria Association.
2. California Penal Code, sections 203, 205.

TWENTY

1. *Standards of Care, Version 1.* 1979. Harry Benjamin International Gender Dysphoria Association.
2. Royal College of Psychiatrists. 2013. *Good Practice Guidelines for the Assessment and Treatment of Adults With Gender Dysphoria.* CR 181. London, Author.
3. *Standards of Care, Version 7.* 2012. World Professional Association for Transgender Health. *International Journal of Transgenderism* 2012, v. 13.

TWENTY-ONE

1. American Psychiatric Association 1980. *Diagnostic and Statistical Manual of* Mental Disorders III. Washington, D.C. Author.
2. Gordon, E. 1991. Transsexual healing: medicaid funding of sex reassignment surgery. *Archives of Sexual Behavior* 20: 61-74.
3. Rabin, R. 2014. Medicare to Now Cover Sex-Change Surgery. *New York Times,* May 30.

TWENTY-TWO

1. In re Grossman 127 N. J. Super. 25, 1974.
2. Ashlie, a/k/a Komarnicki v. Chester-Upland School District, Civil Action 78-4037, D.C., E.D. Penn., May 9, 1979.
3. Green, R. 1978. Sexual identity of 37 children raised by homosexual or transsexual parents. *American Journal of Psychiatry* 135:692-7.
4. C v G (1981) 11 *Family Law* 149 (CA) 49.
5. *Scottish Legal News*. England: Transsexual Fails in Attempt to Have Birth Certificate Changed to Hide Original Gender. 21 April 2015.
6. Title VII, Section 703, Civil Rights Act of 1964 (42 U.S.C. 2000e-2) 1982.
7. Ulane v Eastern Airlines, 581 F. Supp. 821 (N.D. Ill. 1983) reversed 742 F.2d 1081 (7th Circuit 1984)
8. Price Waterhouse v Hopkins 490 US 228, 1989.
9. Green, R. and Fleming, D. 1991. Transsexual Surgery Follow-Up. *Annual Review of Sex Research*. Bancroft, J., Davis, C., and Weinstein, D. editors. Society for the Scientific Study of Sex.
10. A, D, and G v. North West Lancashire Health Authority. 21 December 1998.
11. R. v. North West Lancashire Health Authority. 29 July 1999.

TWENTY-THREE

1. Groskop, V. 2008. My body is wrong. *The Guardian*, 14 August.
2. Green, R. 2008. Response: Young transsexuals should be allowed to put puberty on hold. *The Guardian*, 28 August.

TWENTY-FOUR

1. Hooker, E. 1957. The adjustment of the male overt homosexual. *Journal of Projective Techniques* 21:18-31.

TWENTY-FIVE

1. Money, J. *The Psychologic Study of Man*. Springfield, Ill, Charles C Thomas.
2. Downing, L., Morland, I. and Sullivan, editors. N. 2015. *Fuckology*. Chicago, University of Chicago.
3. Green, R. 1974. *Sexual Identity Conflict in Children and Adults*. New York, Basic Books.
4. Stoller, R. 1973. *Splitting*. New York, Quadrangle.
5. Stoller, R. 1985. *Observing the Erotic Imagination*. New Haven, Yale University Press.
6. Stoller, R. 1979. *Sexual Excitement*. New York, Pantheon.
7. Money, J. 2002. *A First Person History of Pediatric Psychoendocrinology*. New York, Kluwer Academic/Plenum.

8. BBC 2004. Dr. Money and the Boy With No Penis. London, Author.
9. Stoller, R. *Sweet Dreams: Erotic Plots.* London, Karnac.

TWENTY-SIX

1. Dylan, B. 1964. The Times They Are A-Changin'. Copyright 1963, 1964 by Warner Bros. Inc. renewed 1991, 1992 by Special Rider Music.
2. Employment of Homosexuals and Other Sex Perverts in Government. Frontline, Pbs.org
3. Purdom, T. 1995. Clinton Ends Ban on Security Clearance for Gay Workers. *New York Times*, August 4.
4. Rimmerman, C., Wald, K. and Wilcox, C. 2000. *The Politics of Gay Rights*. Chicago, University of Chicago Press.
5. Mooney, l., Knox, D. and Schacht, C. 1993. *Understanding Sexual Politics,* 6th Ed. Wadsworth, Cengage Learning.
6. United States Equal Employment Opportunities Commission. www.eeoc.gov *Advocate* July 16, 2015.
7. The Equality Act 2010. Legislation.gov.uk
8. Truman Signs Code of Service Justice. *New York Times,* May 7, 1950, p 82.
9. GI Bill Turns 62 Today. Military.com. June 22, 2006.
10. *Los Angeles Times*, 1993, July 29.
11. Department of Defense Directive 1304.26
12. House of Representatives 2965, Senate 4023, December 2010.

13. Gays in the military: The UK and US compared. news.bbc. 2 February 2010.

14. DOD Directives 6130.3, 6130.4. Military Standards for Enlistment and Commission Guidelines. Thebalance.com

15. RAND Corporation. 2016. June 30.

16. usatoday.com/story/news/poitics/2011/11/10/more-than-100-troops-seeking-transgender-care/93566330

17. Trump, D. Tweets, July 26, 2017.

18. Carissimo, J. President Obama commutes Chelsea Manning's prison sentence. *Independent,* January 17, 2017.

19. www.Army.Me

20. I am Jazz. TLC network.

21. Bingham, J. Revolution in Attitudes to Homosexuality is Biggest Change in Generation. *The Telegraph*, September 10, 2013.

22. Gallup Poll. www.gallop.com/poll/1651/Gay-Lesbian-Right.aspx

23. Hirsch, A. 2015. Trans People: Poll Reveals Changing Attitudes. News.sky.com

24. Pew Research Center, November 18, 2003. pewforum.org

25. Public Religious Research Institute, November 2011. Strong Majorities Favor Rights and Legal Protection for Transgender People.

26. Smith, T. Son, J. and Kin, J. 2014. Public Attitudes Toward Homosexuality and Gay Rights Across Time and Countries. Williams Institute. law.ucla.edu

Dr. Anonymous. Photo by Kay Tobin, Manuscripts and Archives Division, The New York Public Library.

Ex-GI Becomes Blond Beauty. Daily News front page. New York Daily News Archive, Getty Images.

Christine Comes Home. New York Daily News Archive, Getty Images.

Richard Raskind/Renee Richards. Focus on Sport. Getty Images Sport. Getty Images.

Testifying. Glen Martin. Denver Post. Getty Images.

Singing National Anthem. Photo supplied by Joseph Steffan. Photo by Phil Hoffman.

Springer License 3953041300049. The Three Kings: Harry Benjamin, John Money, Robert Stoller, *Archives of Sexual Behavior* 38:4, 2009.

"The Times They Are A-Changin' " Bob Dylan, 1964, copyright 1963, 1964 by Warner Bros. Inc., renewed 1991, 1992 by Special Rider Music.

Cover: Male Couple. Cake topper designed and made by Sarah Davies-Broadhurst, owner of Miss Cake.

Cover: Male/Female Image. Elenarts/Stock.Adobe. com

Jack Drescher, Jules Black and Pam Elizabeth for commenting on an early draft, Kevin Mills for later editing.

Dagmar Herzog for assistance in obtaining the photo "Testifying".

Jon Davidson for records of the US gay immigration case.

Don Weise, LGBT editor, beneficiary of this history, for re-write pointers.

Paul Posnick, creative artist, for translating my idea of the book cover.

Claire Loveday for providing the title of Section One. And, especially for meticulous badgering to clarify opaque segments throughout the text. With my writing skill, they are now rendered semi-lucid. That was a lot of work. Thank you, Claire.